experiencing God's POWER
for female athletes

dr. deb hoffman with
julie caldwell & kathy schultz

Experiencing God's Power for Female Athletes

Deb Hoffman, Julie Caldwell, and Kathy Schultz

ISBN 1-887002-61-8

Cross Training Publishing
P.O. Box 1541
Grand Island, NE 68802
1-800-430-8588

Copyright © 1999 by Cross Training Publishing

All rights reserved. No part of this book may be reproduced without written permission from the publisher, except by a reviewer who may quote brief passages in a review; nor may any part of this book be reproduced, stored in a retrieval system or transmitted in any form or other without written permission from the publisher.

This book is manufactured in the United States of America.

Library of Congress Cataloging in Publication Data in Progress.

Published by Cross Training Publishing,
P.O. Box 1541
Grand Island, NE 68802

INTRODUCTION

The idea of a Bible study for athletes is nothing new. For years, authors have written material to help athletes develop into individuals who utilize their abilities to glorify God. The unique thing about this particular book is that it focuses exclusively on female athletes. Granted, there are many areas and issues that male and female athletes have in common. Competitiveness, teamwork, athletic performance, and balance are just a few areas that every athlete will deal with at some point in his or her career. However, there are some areas that have not really been addressed and are particular for female athletes, such as identity as a female, stereotypes as a female athlete, and emotional dependency. These types of issues are the primary focus of this book, though the reader will notice other areas that would apply to male athletes as well.

This book is divided into six sections. The first three deal with issues of identity as a Christian, as a female, and as an athlete. The last three sections focus on relationship issues as a Christian, as a female, and as an athlete. This book can be used as an individual study or with a group or partner. It is structured so that you can complete a section on your own prior to a group discussion, or work through it with others. Due to space limitations, it was not possible to include a comprehensive study on every issue presented. Instead, this study is designed to be used as a springboard into more in-depth study of the topics if you so choose. For this purpose, there is an Appendix at the end listing additional books and resources.

Many of the areas written about in this book came as a result of time I spent with various high school and collegiate athletes and coaches. They helped me to identify the current issues that female athletes struggle with the most. Not surprisingly, the issues were, for the most part, the same ones that I experienced or witnessed during my own high school and college days. With the success and attention women have had around the world in athletics in the last several years, the attitude toward women in athletics is very positive and supportive as we head into the new millennium. Hopefully this will result in a proliferation of Bible study materials and books written especially for female athletes, to encourage them as they continue to grow in their relationship with the Lord Jesus and glorify Him through sport.

"Not often, but every once in a while, God brings us to a major turning point–a great crossroads in our life. From that point, we either go toward a more and more slow, lazy, and useless Christian life, or we become more and more on fire, giving our utmost for His highest–our best for His glory."

-Oswald Chambers, My Utmost for His Highest

Foreword

One of the most challenging things to learn in life is to live in the grace of who we really are as females, as athletes, and as followers of Christ. All of these are gifts to be nurtured and explored. This book is for those desiring a deeper understanding of what God calls us to understand about who we are in those roles and how to live accordingly. The authors of this book provide powerful examples of the freedom of living in the grace of these gifts as well as a grasp of what living outside of God's desire for our lives might look like.

This exploration process can be an exciting adventure! In understanding more of who we are as Christians, the authors take us through a process of understanding God's relentless pursuit of us. We learn more about our need for a relationship with Him and our role in the process of growth in that connection. We are encouraged in the areas of prayer and study, and challenged to take a serious look at how this effects relationships with ourselves, others and God.

In understanding who we are as females made in the image of God (Genesis 1:27), and as athletes, they help us take a close look at these in relation to God's desire for us. The reality of the harshness of this world and how that effects our view of ourselves can manifest itself in a variety of ways. Ultimately understanding and interacting with God's view of us is where truth lies. The authors also take us through a process of understanding that our relationships should flow from this truth, and we are given that opportunity with honesty, practicality and balance.

This book is a powerful, interactive tool of discovery. Enjoy the adventure!

Julie Brown
National Director of Programs
Fellowship of Christian Athletes

Contents

1. Identity as a Christian — 9
2. Identity as a Female — 45
3. Identity as an Athlete — 73
4. Relationships as a Christian — 99
5. Relationships as a Female — 123
6. Relationships as an Athlete — 157
   References — 189
   Appendix (Resources) — 193

1
Identity as a Christian

Day 1
The Dream Team (History's Greatest Roster)
Julie was asked to help teach at a high school softball clinic in California. Several players from a local varsity team attended as part of their preseason training. She asked the young women how they thought they would do that season.

"We have a great team!" "We're going to go far this year."

Julie could tell that the players were extremely confident about the success they would have during the season. After hearing the optimism in their voices, she stayed after the clinic was finished to watch the team prepare for its first game of the year. Julie was stunned, to say the least, at what she saw! The girls on the team did not even come close to correctly evaluating their "talent" and had NO idea how good the other teams in their conference were. How could they give a correct estimate of their own abilities without evaluating their competition? What was their standard of measurement?

You may be shocked to hear that many people are like those

athletes...not in regard to sports, but in regard to their lives. Many people base their lives on their own standards and not God's. As a result, inaccurate assumptions are made which will eventually result in a humiliating final record. Are you one of them? In this chapter, we are going to look at the ultimate competition in the game of life and the standard by which our lives are to be lived.

The Ultimate Competition
History's ultimate competition is found in the game of life. In its simplest form, the Bible reveals that God created people, people rejected God, and God won't give up until He wins you back. What's at stake in this competition? A win or loss? Some kind of championship? No. There's a battle for your soul. Your very life is on the line!

God Created People in His Own Image
Despite what you may have learned in school, God created people. When God created you, He had a specific purpose in mind. Read the following verses and write out what you learn about God's purpose for you, His very special creation.

Genesis 1:26-28

Colossians 1:16

1 Corinthians 1:9

Jeremiah 24:7

Identity as a Christian

You were created by God and for God! He has a purpose for your life. God specifically formed you in such a way that you can relate to and know God personally. God is spirit (the Holy Spirit), without a body or physical form (John 4:24), and He designed you in His likeness by giving you a spirit. Have you ever asked yourself questions such as: Who am I? Why am I here? What is the meaning of life? Your spirit is the source of your desires for love, acceptance, and purpose in life. Only God can completely fill the desires of your heart.

God loves you! He creatively expresses His love toward you in many ways, such as giving you the choice to either accept or reject His love. The problem is...

People Rejected God
Genesis 1 tells the story of Adam and Eve, the first humans on earth. When God created Adam and Eve, He made sure they had everything they needed to live. Nothing was missing from their lives! However, God had also given Adam and Eve the ability to make choices. Satan was aware of Adam and Eve's free will (ability to choose), which is an expression of God's love. So Satan tempted Eve. *"'You will not surely die,' the serpent said to the woman. 'For God knows that when you eat of it [the tree] your eyes will be opened, and you will be like God, knowing good and evil'"* (Genesis 3:4, 5). Satan claimed that Adam and Eve did not need God or anyone else to tell them what was right and wrong. He convinced Adam and Eve that they could become their own gods (independent and self-sufficient), and decide for themselves the standards for good and evil.

That is exactly what they chose to do. Adam and Eve doubted God. They decided they would rather try to be self-sufficient instead of trusting their lives to the One who created them, loved them, and gave their lives meaning and purpose. As a result of their disobedience, sin entered the world. God told them, *"In the day that you eat from the tree (of the knowledge of good and evil), you shall surely die"* (Genesis 2:17).

Although Adam and Eve didn't die physically that day, they did die spiritually. God honored their choice to walk in their evil, independent ways and withdrew His life from them.

As a result, all of Adam's offspring (all human beings) are born separated from God! So, when Adam and Eve reproduced a child in their likeness, in their own image, they produced a little sinner! These two spiritually dead parents could not pass on the spiritual life they no longer possessed. Ever since, all men and women have been born spiritually dead, according to the tragic results of Adam and Eve's choice.

Read the following verses and write down what you learn about *your* spiritual condition:

> Romans 3:10-12, 23 (the word "glory" here is used to describe the idea of moral perfection)

> Romans 5:12, 19a; 6:23

> Psalm 51:5

> James 2:10

Identity as a Christian 13

According to the Bible, *everyone* has sinned or missed God's standard of perfection and deserves the punishment of death (eternal separation from God). But because of God's incredible love for you, He still seeks you out. And...

God Won't Give Up Until He Wins YOU Back!
Before the foundation of the world, God knew that Adam and Eve would disobey Him. God, in His ultimate wisdom, had a plan to satisfy the penalty of sin in order to rescue (or "save") you from your spiritual condition (Revelation 13:8). At just the right time, Jesus would leave heaven, be born as a human being, and pay the penalty through *His* death on the cross. Jesus was born in the same way you were (although He was born in a stable and you were probably delivered in a hospital). His mother, Mary, was pregnant with Jesus by the Holy Spirit, not a human father. As a result, although He was 100% human, Jesus was also spiritually alive! This is very important, because since He was spiritually alive, Jesus was able to live His entire life without ever sinning. Jesus made a choice to die for you on the cross.

Jesus took upon Himself ALL the sins of the world, from eternity past to eternity future. God's standard of perfection was satisfied with the offering of Jesus' sinless life, and God raised Jesus from the dead. Satan's grip on death was broken, and all power and authority was returned to Jesus Christ. Once again, people could choose to be spiritually alive, enjoy God's presence, and live with an eternal purpose.

YOU MAKE THE CALL
Remember the varsity team mentioned earlier? Once they faced their competition on the field, they saw their true needs. By then

it was too late to do anything about it, and they finished the season with a 0-12 record.

The truth is that sooner or later you will see Jesus in His holiness, in His power, in His purity. And when that time comes, whether here on earth or when you see Him face to face, you will understand your need for Him as you see yourself for what you truly are. What you'll see isn't lovely at all because your sin is disgusting and repulsive to God. The Apostle Paul cried out, "*I know that nothing good dwells in me, that is, in my flesh...Wretched man that I am! Who will set me free from the body of this death?*" (Romans 7:18, 24). The Good News is that Jesus can and will set you free!

Have you seen your need for God? Unfortunately, there are many influences or attitudes in this "preseason" of life here on earth that might keep you from recognizing your need for the Savior, Jesus Christ. What are they? Is it your natural athletic talent? Your appearance? Your intelligence? Your wealth? Your relationships? Your own righteousness?

   * <u>Who</u> or <u>what</u> keeps you from recognizing your need for God?

God doesn't need your abilities, your beauty, or your brains. God wants your heart! Don't put yourself in the same situation as that varsity team and wait until it is too late to make a decision. The truth is that you need a Savior. You can accurately evaluate your spiritual position by using the ultimate standard of measurement: the Bible. For example, 1 John 5:11, 12 says, *"God has given us eternal life, and this life is in his Son. He who has the Son has life; he who does not have the Son of God does not have life."*

    *According to this verse, where are you in the "game of life"? Do you have the Son?

If you would like to know God personally and allow Jesus Christ to give your life meaning and purpose, in your own words talk to God and do the following:

    *<u>Confess</u> your belief that Jesus Christ is the Son of God, that He died for your sins, was resurrected, and is alive today. (Romans 10:9)
    * <u>Ask</u> God to take control of every area of your life; don't hold anything back.
    * <u>Thank</u> God for allowing you to become His child and for His new life within you.

If you have given God the right to run your life, your name is written on history's greatest roster! Many new and exciting changes have and will continue to take place in your life as you live a great adventure with Him. We'll look at some of these in our next few studies.

Day 2
Your New Position in Christ
Several years ago, an NBA rookie was playing on the Chicago Bulls team with superstar Michael Jordan. Jordan went wild and scored an incredible sixty-eight points during one particular game. The rookie was on the bench until the last minute of the

game, when the coach graciously put him in. The rookie made a single free throw during the final seconds. When he was interviewed afterward, the rookie was very pleased with himself. "Together," he said, "Michael Jordan and I scored sixty-nine points."[1]

So it is in your relationship with the Lord. Together, you and God are unstoppable. You are just a rookie playing with the Legend. As long as He blesses your meager talent, it will be enough. That's exactly what God does when He gives you your position on His team and sends you out. He will take your inadequacies and weaknesses and add His strength. Together you and God can turn the world upside down!

TAKE YOUR POSITION
If you have responded to God's invitation to know Him personally, you are included on history's greatest roster. God says you are "*a new creation; the old has gone, the new has come*" (2 Corinthians 5:17). Today, we are going to take a look at your position in Christ and some of the benefits that are yours when you are identified with God's team.

God has SELECTED you for a new position! "*He chose us in him before the creation of the world to be holy and blameless in his sight. In love, he predestined us to be adopted as his children through Jesus Christ, in accordance with His pleasure and will*" (Ephesians 1:4, 5). You may think that you chose God, but the truth is that He selected you. God personally recruited you to know Him, to love Him, and to serve Him.

Identity as a Christian

Read Romans 8:16-17 and 1 John 3:1-2, then describe this relationship in the space provided below.

Children of God

When you join God's team, you become His child and He becomes your heavenly Father. God selected you to be the recipient of the great exchange as He took your old, dead spirit and replaced it with the life of Jesus Christ. You are a new person. Author Bob George explains the exchange this way:

> "Being made into a 'new creation' is somewhat like the caterpillar that has emerged from its cocoon as a new creature–a butterfly. As a caterpillar, it views life from the ground up. As a butterfly, it views life from the sky downward. In the same way, as a new creature in Christ, you must begin to see yourself as God sees you.
>
> "When one looks at a butterfly, he doesn't say, 'There's a converted worm.' Although it originally was a worm, and it was converted, now it is a butterfly, a beautiful, graceful new creature. The same is true of God. He only sees you as a butterfly–His new creation in Christ.
>
> "Although you may not always act like a 'butterfly,' the truth of the matter is you are never going to be a worm again."[2]

Since you are a new creation, how does God view you? He is a Father who proudly announces your name in His lineup because...

*God KNOWS you (Psalm 139:13-16)
*God deeply LOVES you (John 15:13, 14; 3:16)
*God greatly VALUES you (Romans 5:6-8)
*God DELIGHTS in you (Zephaniah 3:17)

There may be times when you wrestle with believing that God's love for you is this great, but it is true. God not only loves you, He likes you! It seems as though He is "required" to love us, but to enjoy you and to want to spend time with you…? You may tend to look at the ugliness of your sin, but God views you as His child. Even when you seek God's approval, He already says, "I know who you are, my child, and you bring me pleasure." Can you see the smile on Jesus' face as He rejoices over YOU?

God has SECURED your position. *"And you were included in Christ when you heard the word of truth, the gospel of your salvation. Having believed, you were marked in him with a seal, the promised Holy Spirit, who is a deposit guaranteeing our inheritance until the redemption of those who are God's possession–to the praise of his glory"* (Ephesians 1:13, 14).

Have you ever been afraid of losing your position on the team or being replaced in the lineup? Every mistake seems magnified in light of possibly being yanked by the coach, and your confidence seems to dwindle. While this may happen in sports, it doesn't in your relationship with God. That's secure! No mistake is too big to disqualify you from your place on His team.

Read the following verses and write down what proof you have of this secure position.

Identity as a Christian

John 19:28-30

2 Corinthians 1:21, 22

Deuteronomy 31:6, 8; Hebrews 13:5

he will never leave me

Romans 8:35

1 Peter 1:4, 5

When you choose to follow Jesus Christ, the Holy Spirit comes to live in you. He will never leave you. Nothing can separate you from His love. The Holy Spirit is your "proof of purchase" that guarantees your salvation. One of Satan's strategies is to get you to doubt your salvation. But you can be sure that if the spirit of God speaks to your heart, you are God's child (Romans 8:16). Think of the confidence that can be yours as a child who is secure!

God SCHOOLS you at your position. *"I will instruct you and teach you in the way you should go; I will counsel you and watch over you"* (Psalm 32:8).

If you play basketball, how thrilling would it be to have Sheryl Swoopes give you pointers? If you are a soccer player, how would you feel about Mia Hamm helping you to develop your skills? These women are among the best in their sport! Since you are playing in the "game of life," how honored would you be to have God as your "personal trainer"? As one who is trusting in Jesus Christ, that's exactly who you have!! Who better to instruct, direct, and guide you in life than your Creator?! God created you, sees the big picture, and has devised a game plan. Read the following verses about God personally training you.

Jeremiah 31:34

John 14:16-17, 26

Hebrews 13:20, 21

Hebrews 12:7-11

God gives you STRENGTH for your position. *"I pray that out of his glorious riches he may strengthen you with power through his Spirit in your inner being, so that Christ may dwell in your hearts through faith"* (Ephesians 3:16, 17).

God's job is to provide you with all the power, energy, and strength you need to deal with the task at hand. Read 2 Corinthians 9:8 and write it out below.

What is grace? In a nutshell, grace is a relationship of favor that gives you access to God's power. Everything that God is, every-

Identity as a Christian

thing that God has is available to you. According to 2 Peter 1:3, 4, God has given you everything you need for life and godliness.

Take a moment to list what you need to tackle the work God has given you. For example, if you need wisdom, God promises that He will provide it (James 1:5). What is it that you need most right now? Peace? Hope? Trust? Write it down below.

God SEATS you in the best position. *"And God raised us up with Christ and seated us with him in the heavenly realms in Christ Jesus in order that in the coming ages he might show the incomparable riches of his grace, expressed in his kindness to us in Christ Jesus"* (Ephesians 2:6). Do you realize that you have the best seat in the house? God has seated you in heaven with Christ. He wants to give you His perspective on life.

Julie traveled to Switzerland one year. As she drove through the valleys of the Swiss Alps, she was amazed at how majestic those mountains looked. One afternoon she went with two of her friends to a spot known as the "Top of Europe," where she could see one enormous mountain range after another. The view was absolutely spectacular! From that vantage point, she was barely able to fix her eyes on one of the ranges she had noticed from the valley. Suddenly her perspective completely changed. She noticed the mountain that once looked gigantic was, in fact, tiny in comparison to the surrounding peaks.

There may be something in your life that seems like a mountain looming in front of you—an injury, a troubled relationship, poor grades, financial difficulties. It may be something you need

God's perspective on. Write down one or two of the "mountains" you are facing today. God wants to reveal His ways to you through His Word. Read Isaiah 55:8. Ask God to give you His perspective on it, then watch to see God's answer to your request.

So, what do you think of your position on God's team? Imagine the confidence you can have as a woman who is selected by God, secure in your relationship with Him, schooled by the Spirit of God, strengthened to abound in every good work, and seated in the heavenlies with Christ!! It sounds like you're dressed for success!

Day 3
Taking it to the Next Level–Growing in Christ
How often are you and most athletes you know content with a good performance? It seems never! Athletes naturally strive to take their performance to another level as they fine-tune their fundamental skills. The coaches of the 1996 U.S. gold medal Olympic softball team expressed that one of the greatest needs of softball players at all levels is to improve their ability to execute the bunt. Imagine that! The best players in the world have to work on the fundamentals.

Is the same true for you? Do you look for ways to improve your game? Choose one of the skills in your sport and think about what you were like as a player one year ago. Now ask yourself a few questions:

* How have you improved your ability to perform that skill?

* What have you done to increase your physical conditioning?

*Has your knowledge of the game improved? How?

As an athlete, it is almost second nature to push yourself to the limit to reach your goals. But have you thought about taking your *spiritual fitness* to the next level?

This time, think about where you were *spiritually* one year ago, and answer the following questions in regard to your spiritual growth:

* In what areas have you grown spiritually?

*What have you done to improve your spiritual fitness?

*Has your knowledge and understanding of God increased? In what ways?

If you are at the same skill level as an athlete that you were a year ago, your coach would have reason to be concerned. If you are at the same place in your Christian walk that you were a year ago, you better be careful! You might be wise to get a "checkup" on your spiritual health!

Work Out Your Salvation
God wants you to mature in your relationship with Him. He is calling you to work out (not work for) your salvation so that you can love Him with all your heart and be a reflection of His character (Romans 8:29).

Read the following verses and put into your own words what you are encouraged to do to grow spiritually:
   1 Peter 2:2

   2 Peter 3:18

   Hebrews 6:1, 2

   Philippians 2:12-16

God expects us to grow in our salvation. How do we do that? Oswald Sanders, in his book *Enjoying Intimacy With God*, writes, "Everything in our Christian life and service flows from our relationship with God. If we are not in vital fellowship with Him, everything else will be out of focus."[3] Spiritual growth begins by spending time with God, because a relationship of any depth takes time.

Identity as a Christian

TIME OUT!
The pressure is on! Have you ever noticed what a coach does when the momentum seems to swing in favor of the other team? Or what happens when everything seems to go wrong at the same time? What action will your coach take? What can you do as an athlete? Call time out!

> * What is the purpose of a time out?

Time outs are necessary to take a step back from a pressure situation, to refocus on the task at hand, to develop a strategy, to look at the "big picture."

Time is a valued commodity these days. School, sports, friends, family, church, and work seem to demand so much of your time and emotional energy that there aren't enough hours in a day to do it all. Yet, if time outs are beneficial and often times necessary for success in athletics, how much more important is it for you to step outside your daily routine to grow in your relationship with God?

In order to develop this relationship, you must be alone and quiet before Him so that you will know how you can and are to live! Spending time alone with God as often as possible is not an obligation; it is a necessity! It is not for reward or blessing that you must be alone with Him, but for life. People often refer to the time set aside in their schedule to deepen their relationship with God a "quiet time." Scripture never mentions the words "quiet time," yet the Bible gives us many examples of men and women who spent time alone with God.

Jesus' Example

The supreme example is always found in our Lord Jesus Christ, who often spent time alone with God the Father. If Jesus, who was God in the flesh, found it necessary to be alone with God, how much more do we need to be still and listen to God? Jesus' life consisted of *total dependence* upon the Father and is the example for us to follow. Jesus did nothing on His own initiative, but only spoke as the Father taught Him, only doing those things that were pleasing to Him (John 8:28, 29). If Jesus lived in this kind of dependence on God, can we really serve Him by having any less of a relationship with our Heavenly Father (Luke 5:16; 6:12; Mark 1:35; Matthew 14:23; John 17:4)?

Your Utmost Priority

Life is based on relationships, so one of the keys to spending time alone with the Lord is deciding how much time you want to devote to developing your relationship with God. God leaves that up to you. He is there–always available, always waiting.

It is also important to understand that the greater the pressure, the greater your need for time alone with Him. Is it any wonder that so many people crumble under the stress and pressure of the world when so few have made their relationship to God the utmost priority of their life?

With that in mind, take a moment or two to think about what kind of relationship you would like to have with God. Based on your decision, determine what you need to do in each of the following areas. Write your answers in the space provided.

* How long will your quiet time be? Five, fifteen, sixty minutes?

Identity as a Christian

* How often will you have your quiet time? Once a week, a few times a week, once a day?

* When is the best time for you? In the morning, afternoon, or evening?

Determine to make this time with God a priority. Draw upon His grace to meet with Him consistently. During this time you can worship God, talk and listen to Him, and study His Word. Make these fundamentals a regular part of your time with Him and see what happens. We will take a closer look at each of these fundamentals in the next two sections.

More Than Just an Appointment
Scheduling a time out or quiet time with God regularly is well worth the commitment. However, your relationship with God is much deeper than a daily appointment. One unique characteristic about God is that He is always with you. As you become more aware of His presence, you can enjoy fellowship with Him throughout the day. One way to remind yourself that God is present is to set your watch to chime every hour. When the watch chimes, take a moment or two to tell the Lord that you love Him and ask Him if you are living in a way that is pleasing to Him. You can also write out verses on index cards. Place the cards somewhere so that you can read them as a reminder throughout the day that God is with you, longing to love you and be involved with every aspect of your life.

Fitness Checkup

1. If God were to give you a spiritual checkup, what kind of spiritual condition would He say you are in right now?

2. Is God the ultimate priority in your life? Is there anything you need to change in order to consistently meet with Him and deepen your relationship with Him?

3. What are some things you can do to become more aware of God's presence throughout the day?

Day 4
Radical Rap–A Prayer Workout
Have you ever watched a sporting event and noticed what happens when there is a lack of communication during the game? The coach calls for a full-court press during a time out, but one player is in the wrong position and the other team scores an easy lay-up. Or the setter puts the ball high and outside, but the hitter is expecting the ball to be inside and close to the net and is swinging at air as she realizes the mistake. Maybe you've seen the coach give the signal for a bunt and the runner is caught off guard because she wasn't paying attention. Communication is important not just in sports, but in life. In this section we are going to take a closer look at prayer, our way of communicating with God.

Listening to the Coach
What would happen if your coach stopped speaking to your team during a game? Confusion. Frustration. Mistakes. Instead,

Identity as a Christian

your coach interacts with the team to give instruction, direction, and encouragement so you can experience success.

Communication is obviously important in sports, but even more important in your relationship with God! Since God has a specific plan for your life (Ephesians 2:10), you would greatly benefit from spending time with Him to receive instruction, direction, and encouragement. Not only that, but when two people are in love they spend time sharing with one another and enjoying each other's company. Our relationship with God should be no different. Unfortunately, we often spend more time talking about prayer than actually doing it.

It is a radical thought that we can call God "Father," and we have direct access to speak with Him 24/7: twenty-four hours a day, seven days a week. In its simplest form, prayer is two-way communication between you and God. It involves talking to *and* listening to God like you would with a friend, yet is different because God is the Creator of the whole universe!

Prayer Fitness

Although most of us aren't "pros" in prayer, we would probably agree that prayer is important and we want to be more effective in prayer. So how do you pray? What do you pray? When do you pray? That is what Jesus' disciples were asking when they said, "Lord, teach us to pray."

Pastor Bill Hybels writes, "Developing prayer fitness is like developing physical fitness: you need a *pattern* to avoid becoming imbalanced. Without a routine, you will probably fall into the 'Please God' trap: 'Please God, give me. Please God, help me. Please God, cover me. Please God, arrange this.'"[4]

* What kind of pattern, if any, do you use?

When someone teaches you a skill in a sport, the best way to learn and improve is to practice that skill. Therefore, instead of just talking about prayer, we are going to learn about prayer by praying.

If prayer is something new or undeveloped in your life, think back to what it was like when you took up a new sport or learned a new skill. When you tried it the first time you probably felt clumsy, unsure, or uncomfortable. As you spent time practicing, you became more comfortable with it. The same is true of prayer. As you take the time to "practice," you will grow.

Practicing Prayer

Jesus gave us easy step-by-step instructions for a balanced and comprehensive plan to develop the skill of prayer. Take a moment to read His instructions, found in Matthew 6:9-15 (this passage is often referred to as "the Lord's Prayer").

In her book, *Lord, Teach Me To Pray*, Kay Arthur explains that each sentence in the Lord's Prayer touches on a topic of worship, allegiance, submission, provision, confession, and protection that can lead you into deeper conversation with God.[5]

[Worship]	"Our Father in heaven, hallowed be your name,
[Allegiance]	your kingdom come,
[Submission]	your will be done, on earth as it is in heaven.
[Provision]	Give us today our daily bread.
[Confession]	Forgive us our debts, as we also have forgiven our debtors.
[Protection]	And lead us not into temptation, but deliver us from the evil one."

Identity as a Christian 31

Whether you have ten minutes or an hour, you are able to cover the entire range of subjects which Jesus teaches are important to communication with God.

Are you ready to touch the heart of God and move His hand? Are you ready to be changed?

"Our Father in heaven, hallowed be your name..."
As you begin your time of prayer, direct your focus to your heavenly Father who loves you, cares for you, and longs to spend time with you. Maybe one of the following ideas will help as you spend time in worship.

> *Exalt His name. Understand God for who He is and tell Him of His worth-ship as you ponder and proclaim one of His names (e.g. Father, Creator, Counselor, Sovereign Lord...)
> *Lift Him up through the Word. A good place to start is the book of Psalms (i.e. chapters 8, 9, 19, 24, 29, 30, 33-35, 47, 48, 65, 66, 68).
> *Praise Him through a song. Use songs you sing at church or youth group.

"Your kingdom come..."
Once you recognize God for who He truly is–the One to be worshiped and the One who rules over all–the next step would be to bow your heart to Him. People and things compete for first place in our lives. It's easy to think that things like money (treasures), abilities (talents), time, and your body (temple) are your own, but God has entrusted these to you to be used for His glory.

As you continue praying, examine your heart and submit yourself to God so that He has first place in all areas of your life.

* Treasures. Are your family, finances, friends, goals, ambitions, and everything else in your life submitted to God?
* Talents. Does God get the glory as you play your sport? Is He honored when you play the game? Through your gifts and abilities?
* Time. Do you allow God to direct your time? How do you spend your time?
* Temple. Are you honoring God by taking care of your body? Do you speak words of encouragement to others? Do your thoughts please the Lord?

"Your will be done on earth as it is in heaven..."
Submit to the will of God. Recognize that you're not coming to God on your own terms, but HIS. How do you understand His will? By renewing your mind through the Word of God (Romans 12:1, 2). To pray the will of God is to pray the Word of God!

Take a moment to let the Lord know that you want His will to be done more than your own.

"Give us this day our daily bread..."
Now that you've worshiped your heavenly Father, affirmed your allegiance to God, and submitted your will to Him, you are ready to ask for your daily needs. Time will go by quickly as you begin asking God to provide those daily needs that sustain life. The following ideas may help you pray more effectively:

Identity as a Christian

* Pray with faith (Matthew 9:28; Mark 11:22-24)
* Pray with direction from the whole counsel of God (1 John 5:14, 15)
* Pray specifically (John 17:15-21)
* Pray largely and broadly (Jeremiah 33:3; Acts 4:29, 30)
* Pray with passionate spiritual desire (1 Samuel 1:10, 11)
* Pray persistently (Luke 11:5-13)
* Pray with a listening ear for God (Psalm 40:6, 8)
* Pray through a prayer list, and journal your prayers (Psalms)

Below is an example of how you can keep track of your prayers:

<u>Request</u>   <u>Date Answered</u>

You
_____
_____
_____
_____

Your family
_____
_____
_____

Key people in your life (i.e. friends, teammates, roommates)
_____
_____
_____
_____

The nation (i.e. national, state and local leaders, pastor)

_____
_____
_____
_____

The World (i.e. missionaries, the persecuted church)

_____
_____
_____
_____

"Forgive us our debts, as we also have forgiven our debtors..." While asking for our needs may not be hard to do, confessing our sins is an area that we often forget about or ignore. It is important to give the Holy Spirit time to reveal sin in your lives so that we can receive His forgiveness and reestablish our fellowship with Him. Take some time now to quiet yourself before the Lord and...

> * Ask God to forgive you of the thoughts, attitudes, actions, and words that are contrary to His holiness (e.g. pride, disobedience, fear, sexual immorality, unkindness, judgment of others, complaining, self-pity, ungratefulness, jealousy, bitterness, filthy language, lack of discipline, etc.).
> * Ask God to replace those areas in our life with genuine Christ-likeness (humility, obedience, love, purity, self-control, kindness, thankfulness, forgiveness, etc.).

Identity as a Christian

* Accept God's grace and draw upon it to give to others the same forgiveness you have just received. Forgive anyone with whom you are angry, upset, offended, etc.

"For if you forgive men when they sin against you, your heavenly Father will also forgive you. But if you do not forgive men their sins, your Father will not forgive your sins" (Matthew 6:14, 15).

"Lead us not into temptation, and deliver us from the evil one..."
This prayer is the heart-cry of a child of God who is aware that "the spirit is willing, but the flesh is weak." As you seek to stand right before God make sure that you do the following.

* Ask God to keep you from the sins and temptations that tend to cause you to fall.

* Pray for God's protection from the schemes of the enemy.

FINISHING WELL
Perhaps you are convicted and desire to do something about your prayer life, but you are discouraged because of past experiences. You seem to start out strong but fizzle out. If so, you might have forgotten one of the most important ingredients: we need GRACE to keep on praying (Hebrews 4:16; James 4:5, 6). Ask God every day for His grace to pray.

Fitness Checkup
1. If God were to give you a spiritual checkup today, how fit would you be in the area of prayer? What are your strengths in prayer? What are your weaknesses?

2. Prayer isn't just something to check off your "to-do" list. Prayer helps you to draw near to God and to develop your relationship with Him. Make prayer a priority. Decide on a specific time and place to meet with God every day (Mark 1:35). Write it below.

Day 5
Running the Race to Win–God's Playbook for Life
In the last section, we looked at the importance of growing in our relationship with God through prayer. Now we will look at how we can take this relationship to the next level by studying the Bible, God's word to us.

If you decided that you wanted to learn about soccer, you could use one of two methods. One would be to go to the library and check out all the books about soccer. You could then read them and find out what each different author had to say about soccer. When the authors disagreed, you would have to try and decide who was right. This could all be done without ever touching a soccer ball!

The other way to go about your research would be to go down to the soccer field and watch a game, or even get a "feet-on" experience. You could watch others play the game, learn the rules, pick up on some of the basic skills and strategies, etc. When you were finished, you could even go home and practice what you just saw! You would then have firsthand experience with soccer and would know for sure that your information was accurate. It would take more time and effort than just reading

Identity as a Christian

about soccer, but you would not quickly forget what you had seen and experienced for yourself.

Studying the Word of God
"Man does not live on bread alone, but on every word that comes from the mouth of God" (Matthew 4:4).

Have you ever wondered what God is really like? Study the Bible. Would you like to know who you are, why you are here, or what the meaning of life is? You can find the answers in the Bible. Do you ever wonder what God has to say about certain issues such as image, drugs and alcohol, premarital sex, loneliness, suicide, and many other relevant topics? The Bible is your "playbook" for life. God wants to guide you, protect you, and bring you success.

> * If you could ask God anything, what would you like to know?

Read the following verses about the Bible and put into your own words what God says about this special book, which is unlike any other book ever written.

> 2 Timothy 3:16, 17

> 2 Peter 1:19-21

> 2 Samuel 22:31

Hebrews 4:12

John 17:17

Psalm 119:105

Through the Bible, God reveals Himself, His purposes, and His ways. Every word is flawless and lights your path with the truth. His word is alive, active, and practical for your daily life. In order to discover truths such as these for yourself, you will need to read the Bible in such a way that will help you determine the following:

* What the Bible says (observation)

* What the Bible means (interpretation)

* How to apply the Bible to your life (application)

This is called the *inductive* method of study. It is one of the best ways to study the Bible because it takes you directly to the Bible itself. This method doesn't tell you what the Bible means or what you should believe. Instead, it helps you to understand and know the Bible by showing you how to see what it says for yourself. Once you see what the Bible says, you can understand its meaning and put that meaning into practice in your own life. This, of course, is the goal of Bible study: to be transformed by the Word of God and to develop a closer relationship with God.

Strategic Study

Are you ready to learn how to study the Word of God? Let's start by using the inductive method to study 1 Corinthians 9:24-27.

1. Begin your time with prayer. Ask the Holy Spirit to teach you (John 16:13-15).

2. Choose a book or paragraph from the Bible (for this example we are using 1 Corinthians 9:24-27). Read the entire passage 3-5 times to get a good grasp on what the author is trying to say.

3. Read the passage again, this time asking the following questions as you read: Who? What? Where? When? Why? and How?

Who? Who wrote it? Who was he writing to? Who are the main characters?

What? What are the main events? What is the meaning of the message? What are these people like? What is the author's purpose in saying this?

When? When was this written? When did this event happen, or when will it take place?

Where? Where was this written? Where was this done? Where will it happen?

Why? Why did the author say so much (or so little) about this? Why did God want me to know this? What point was the author trying to make to the people he is writing to?

How? How did it happen? How did they do it? How do I do that?

Record your answers in the space provided or in a notebook. You will be amazed at how much you learn, and how much is in the Bible that you didn't know was there!

Hints to Enhance Your Study

* Find out the context. This is very important to correctly interpret the passage. For example, according to *Webster's New World Dictionary*, the following definitions are given for the word "slide":

1. A smooth, often inclined, surface for sliding
2. A photographic transparency for use with a projector or viewer
3. A small glass plate on which objects are mounted for microscopic study
4. The fall of a mass of rock, snow, etc. down a slope.

The context of the sentence will determine which meaning you use!

* Look for the obvious. Facts about people, places, and events will often be repeated, making them easy to see.

They provide you with a framework for the text.

> * Be objective. Let Scripture speak for itself; don't try to make it say what you've always thought it said. Ask God to make His truth obvious to you and then adjust your life accordingly.

How important is it to study the Bible? It is so important that you should schedule your day around your time in the Word instead of squeezing your time in the Word around your schedule!

Fitness Checkup
1. If God were to give you a spiritual fitness checkup today, how fit would you be in the area of knowing the Word of God? What are your strengths in this area? What are your weaknesses?

2. Decide on a specific time and place where you will meet with God and allow Him to speak to you through His Word, the Bible. Be consistent in your time with Him and "listen" to what He wants to teach you!

Team Applause–Building One Another Up
So far, we've looked at the importance of prayer and Bible study. There is another fundamental skill that you need to develop in order to grow in the knowledge and grace of our Lord Jesus Christ: fellowship.

Have you ever been to a sporting event and cheered for the visiting team? Not long into the game it occurs to you that you might be the only fan in the crowd. You'd be wise to keep quiet, but you are so excited you burst out in a cheer for YOUR team.

People begin to turn and look at you. That's when you notice you have a friend across the aisle. She, too, applauds the visiting team. When you clap, she claps. As you shout, she shouts. You have a partner, and suddenly you don't feel so alone anymore! You are united with a common purpose.

The church (not a building, but Christians) helps you to not feel alone. All week you cheer for the visiting team. You applaud the One the world opposes. You stand when everyone sits and sit when everyone stands. At some point you need support. You need to be with the people who cheer when you do. You need what the Bible calls *fellowship*, and you need it on a regular basis. After all, if you don't have support you may start to feel pressured to join the crowd (the world).

Fellowship
"Let us not give up meeting together, as some are in the habit of doing, but let us encourage one another" (Hebrews 10:25).

Read the following verses and write out what you learn about the importance of having fellowship with other Christians.

1 John 1:7

1 Corinthians 12:12-31

1 Thessalonians 5:11

Identity as a Christian

Just as your athletic team could not make it without a point guard (or pitcher, setter, or goalie), Christians need each other. You need to fellowship with Christians, and they need to fellowship with you. God has uniquely gifted each of us to build each other up in Christ. Are you doing your part?

Fitness Checkup

Do you consistently get together with other Christians for fellowship (i.e. local church, campus ministry, Bible study)? If not, what can you do to obey God's Word in Hebrews 10:25?

2
Identity as a Female

Day 1
Made in God's Image
Genesis 1:27 states, *"God created man in his own image, in the image of God he created him; male and female he created them."* In the first part of the verse, "God created man in his [God's] own image," the word for man is *adam*, meaning humankind. This refers to all people. The expression "image of God" (*imago Dei*) refers to how God is reflected, or seen, in people. Males and females both reflect the image of God.

What do you think it means to be made in the image of God?

The image of God is something that all humans possess (Genesis 9:6, James 3:9-10). Jesus Christ is Himself the visible representation and manifestation of God to created beings (Colossians 1:15). Although the first humans (Adam and Eve) were intended to be a perfect representation of the image of God, sin corrupted that image in some way. Still, all people have inherent dignity and worth since we somehow reflect the image of God. The Bible clearly states two ways that people reflect the image of God: in **accountable authority** and in **morality**.

In Genesis 1:28-30, God gives humans dominion (authority) over the rest of creation. This means that people have authority over animals, plants, the environment, etc., and are supposed to care for creation as well as use it to survive. People are accountable to God regarding how they use (or misuse) their authority.

In 2 Corinthians 3:18, Paul writes, *"We, who with unveiled faces all reflect the Lord's glory."* The word "glory" in this passage refers to the Hebrew sense of morality; that is, holiness, righteousness, and truth. God has perfect morality. All people possess a sense of morality, although the degree of morality may differ greatly between individuals or cultures. Paul further states that this glory cannot be fully restored in humans by following the law (commandments), but is restored through Jesus Christ. Remember that Jesus was without sin. He was morally perfect. Jesus Christ is the image of God. As Christians we are in the process of continuing to become like Jesus. However, we will not be complete in His image until Jesus returns to establish His kingdom.

There are other ways that people reflect the image of God. Although they are not stated explicitly, we can infer from the Scriptures the following:

Creativity. God is the ultimate Creator (Genesis 1). People reflect God's creativity in many ways: song, art, dance, architecture, and writing, to name a few. No other creature is able to reflect the creative powers of the Almighty God in the way humans do.

Rationality. Compared to the rest of creation, humans have the capacity to reason, to think. This ability also allows us to know

God on a deeper level than the rest of creation. (Psalm 8:3; 143:5; Luke 12: 27).

Relationship. Just as the members of the Trinity (God, Jesus, and the Holy Spirit) relate to one another (Genesis 1), people reflect this quality in human relationships. The relationships that can best reflect this quality can include friendships between individuals and within the church. In fact, as Christians, one way we are to draw unbelievers to God is by demonstrating His love in our relationships with each other.

Spirituality. People have the ability to relate not only to one another, but also to God. This means that we are unique from the animals, who do not possess the ability to have a relationship with God in the way humans do.

All people bear the image of God, and yet on earth we are limited in our ability to reflect that image in the way originally intended. Just as the divine glory is manifest in every person to some degree, there is a dignity that accompanies the divine glory. All human life is sacred. Even a severely handicapped person who is not able to think or respond in the ways others do is no less in the image of God. Every person falls short of the glory of God (Romans 3:23). The image of God will be fully restored in every Christian when Christ returns (Revelation 20:4). Only in heaven will we achieve the purpose for which humankind was originally created: to worship God for eternity (Revelation 5:11-13). Non-Christians are also in the image of God, but they cannot be fully restored in the image of God except through Christ. Non-Christians will not be resurrected and glorified when Christ returns. Instead, they will be eternally tormented (Revelation 20:11-15). That is a sobering thought!

It was mentioned earlier that the image of God in humans was somehow tarnished when sin entered the world, but it was not completely destroyed (Genesis 5:1-3; James 3:9). We no longer display the image of God in the perfect, holy way that God originally planned. As humans we sin, and sometimes in our sin we cause harm to others. There is much evidence of a tarnished image in the world today, and we will consider this evidence in the studies for Days 3 and 4. For now, let's consider the ways that the image of God is present in you as a female.

Seeing the Image through Imagery

Very often, the masculine gender is used to refer to God (e.g. He, Him, His). This does not mean that God is a male. When "He" is used in reference to God, it is because in the English language the masculine pronoun is sometimes used generically to refer to all human beings. The Bible also uses imagery to describe God. Imagery is a way to help us understand what God is like in His character and to enable us to relate to Him. Deuteronomy 4:15-16 says that since God cannot be seen, it is wrong to assume that we can make an image of God that will resemble what God looks like. Imagery can help us as we attempt to understand God and His character, but imagery does not define who God is or what God looks like.[1] The Bible also uses feminine imagery to describe God. Read the following passages and write down the word or phrase used to describe God.

Exodus 34:6-7

Isaiah 66:13

Matthew 23:37

There are other important aspects to your identity as a female. You are created in a way that allows you to experience a variety of emotions. Your feelings and emotions allow you to experience depth in relationships. Emotions are not "bad" or "good." Emotions have no value; they are a part of our experience as humans. However, we are encouraged to have self-control and not allow our emotions to produce negative or harmful results. For example, Ephesians 4:26 says, *"In your anger do not sin: Do not give the devil a foothold."* Although there will be times when you feel angry about something that has happened, you are not to let your anger take control and lead to negative or harmful results such as hatred or bitterness. You are to take responsibility over your own emotions (Proverbs 29:11) and not intentionally provoke emotions like anger in other people (Proverbs 15:1, 30:33).

In the movie "A League of their Own," actor Tom Hanks plays the role of a former major league player who becomes the coach of an all-female baseball team. During one scene, he yells at one of the players for making a costly mistake during the game. She starts to cry. He stares at her in disbelief and screams, "What are you doing? There's no crying in baseball!" Although meant to be humorous, this scene is typical of the confusing messages sometimes given to women regarding feelings. Comments such as "big girls don't cry" or "you've got to be tough like the boys if you're gonna play this game" teach girls that they cannot have feelings or show emotions and also be successful athletes.

Consider the emotions of Jesus described in the Bible. They are an indication of Jesus' humanity and ability to understand how we are feeling. Read the following verses and write down the emotions Jesus experienced:

John 2:13-17

John 11:32-36

Mark 14:32-34

Mark 14:37-41

Luke 13:34

Luke 22:44

Matthew 14:14

Matthew 9:35

Keep in mind that if Jesus experienced emotions and was without sin, then it is not a sin to experience emotions! You may have

Identity as a Female

been taught that it is wrong or unacceptable to experience certain feelings.

Is it difficult for you to share your emotions with others? If so, why?

You can accept your feelings and emotions as part of who God created you to be. He desires that your emotions be used to relate to Him and others, not "stuffed" away as if they do not exist.

When the Pharisees asked Jesus what the greatest commandment was, He replied, "Love the Lord your God with all your heart and with all your soul and with all your mind" (Matthew 22:37). The word for "heart" in some cases can translate "the seat of human emotions." You are to use your emotional capacity to love God with everything you have! Take a moment and reflect on your relationship with God.

TIME OUT!
As a review, write down what it means to be made in the image of God.

Day 2
Have you ever stopped and thought about what it means to be female? Psalm 139 describes how God knew you before you were even born, while you were still in your mother's womb. God knew what gender you were going to be, and He is pleased that you are female! You are special because you were created female.

Males and females are different in many ways. Hormones allow you to develop primary (internal sex organs) and secondary (breast development, distribution of body hair) sex characteristics that are different from those of males. There are many differences that may not be biological in nature, but are still characteristic of men and women. Women often are more social and demonstrate a stronger need for relationships. Men are often quite task-driven and may not express as great a need for emotional closeness as women. Some of these differences may be a result of socialization, or conditioning. It used to be thought that certain activities were best left to men, such as sports. Women were better equipped (or so it was thought) to be in the kitchen. Times have changed! Obviously, there are some differences that do not change because they are inherent–both genders have those differences. Some differences, on the other hand, are taught or modeled to us and may change over time.

The field of neuroscience (study of the brain) also demonstrates male-female differences. Neuroscience reveals that human brains have two sides, a left hemisphere and a right hemisphere. The two sides look very similar, but each has specific functions. For most people, the left hemisphere of the brain tends to focus on language, logical analysis, mathematics, and other analytic activities that involve thinking through steps or a pattern to solve problems. The right hemisphere is most often used for artistic and spatial abilities, and for emotional, non-analytic, and non-verbal approaches to problems.[2] This does not mean that only the left side of the brain is used for some functions and the right side of the brain is only used for others. Generally, most people usually have one side of the brain that is more effective for certain activities than the other. Some researchers believe that men's brains tend to be more specialized; that is, the abili-

Identity as a Female

ties for certain tasks, such as mathematics, occur most strongly in one hemisphere of the brain (the left). Females, however, seem to have a greater ability to use both hemispheres for some functions.

This does not mean that women are better than men, or vice versa. The differences between males and females were meant to complement each other. Unfortunately, society often turns those differences into a competition. God designed males and females to be different in some ways and similar in others. Whether as a result of biology, conditioning, or a combination of both, overall women seem to have a greater capacity to communicate on an emotional level than men. This is not to say that men don't have emotions, but rather women are much more likely to "be in touch" with their emotions and to share them with others.

What are some other differences that you've noticed between males and females, especially in regard to communication and relationships?

Females	Males

Your Feminine Side

We can't have a discussion about what it means to be female

without an understanding of femininity. What does it mean to be feminine? Does it mean that you have to wear pink bows in your hair, lace on your skirt, and learn to sew? No. Those things themselves do not make a person feminine. Femininity has more to do with the inward attitude toward yourself. For some women, that's hard to do. If you were ever teased about your looks, or ever felt insecure about being a female, you may not have a very positive attitude about yourself or your gender.

Look at the characteristics listed below. Place an "M" beside those qualities you think of as masculine, and an "F" beside those qualities you think of as feminine.

____Assertive   ____Caring   ____Intelligent

____Supportive   ____Aggressive   ____Athletic

____Encouraging   ____Relational   ____Creative

____Strong   ____Nurturing   ____Courageous

____Protective   ____Gentle   ____Trustworthy

Actually, each of these qualities can describe both males and females. The way in which these qualities are demonstrated by men and women may differ. One author writes that both men and women have a combination of masculine and feminine traits, but women have more emphasis on the feminine ones. She defines feminine traits as soft, yielded, responsive, nurturing, and receptive, while masculine traits are those that are decisive and assertive. This is not to say that women are not decisive or

Identity as a Female

assertive, but often those traits look somewhat different in men and women. She also states that femininity is "the essence of what God intends women to think, feel, and act like. A truly feminine woman honors God in all these aspects of her life."[3]

Remember the previous lesson on what it means to be in the image of God? Genesis 1:27 tells us that God possesses all masculine and feminine qualities. God is a perfect combination of masculine and feminine. God created men and women differently so that they would complement each other and accurately reflect who God is. One gender is not superior to the other.

Day 3
There is a crisis in America today. A crisis of morals, of violence, of young people hurt by or getting involved in activities they are not physically, emotionally, or spiritually prepared to handle. Here is an idea of what is happening to young people today in the United States. Every day in the U.S. the following occurs:
* 500 adolescents begin using drugs
* 1,000 adolescents begin drinking alcohol
* 3,610 teens are assaulted, 80 are raped
* 1,000 unwed teenage girls become mothers
* 1,106 teenage girls get an abortion
* 135,000 kids take a gun or other weapon to school
* 7 kids (ages 10-19) are murdered
* 6 teenagers commit suicide[4]

What kind of effect do these events have on an individual? A tremendous effect! Many young people today are so angry that they no longer care what effect their behavior will have on others or themselves. Your behavior indicates your true beliefs about yourself. We believe what we are told about who we are by the people most important to us. If you were raised in a home where you were constantly told that you were worthless, unwanted, and a burden, chances are you believe these things about yourself. You may turn your feelings of pain and anger inward and develop a "tough" exterior, not letting others get close to you, all to protect yourself from getting hurt again.

The Tarnished Image
In the first chapter, we saw how all people fall short of God's standard. God wants a relationship with us so that we might enjoy eternal life with Him and that our lives on earth are all that He intends for us. Sadly, we live in a sinful world where the decisions made by us or others can negatively impact us and our relationship with Christ. For many young women, the image of God as a loving father is difficult to fathom because their earthly fathers did not care about them, abused them, ignored them, or were not even involved in their lives. To think of God as Father is not something these women can do easily. In fact, it may even be difficult for them to believe that God is real, available, and that He wants a relationship with them. However, God is a perfect Father. Scripture says that God is *"A father to the fatherless, a defender of widows, is God in his holy dwelling. God sets the lonely in families"* (Psalm 68:5-6). Even if your earthly family did not fulfill its responsibility to provide a loving, safe, and nurturing place for you to grow, God desires for you to experience that among a different family, the family of Christians (Mark 3:33).

When the image you have of yourself is tarnished, you may have difficulty believing that God accepts you for who you are, even though things may have happened in the past. You may blame yourself that someone else abused you, or left you, or treated you poorly. You may believe that God would not accept you if He knew of all the horrible things that have happened in your life. You may even blame God for what others have done to you. What things from the past still have you shaking your fist at God?

Do you have a difficult time thinking of God as a loving Father?

God does not cause or want evil to happen (John 3:20, James 1:13, 14). Read the following passage and write down what Jesus told His disciples about those who would harm children or cause them to sin.

Luke 17:1-2

Debbie Haliday, an FCA staff member in Southern California, once spoke at a conference on the idea of God as our father. It is like God is your dad and you're a little girl again, and sometimes things happen that you don't like, or you get angry about, and you are so mad that you run up to God and shout, "Why did you let this happen?" and you flail your small arms at him, throwing a tantrum, wanting him to know you hurt. And God, like the good Father that He is, stands and lets you express your anger to Him while He slowly bends over, wraps you up in His loving arms, and holds you close to Him until the anger subsides. God already knows about everything that has happened in the past. He is aware of everything that you have ever done or thought as well as what others might have done to you. Remember from Chapter 1 that God will forgive us of the sin in our lives. There is no sin that can keep us from a relationship with Him. He accepts us as we are, but He does want us to deal with the effects of sin in our lives so that we may develop our identity as His child.

Sometimes it is not a sin that we have a problem with, but the effects of a sin. For example, a girl who is abused did not commit any sin. She did not cause the abuse to happen. But she will most likely suffer effects from the abuse that someone else committed, such as difficulty trusting others, or a sense of shame or guilt about her body. These are obstacles that prevent her from growing spiritually.

"But one thing I do: Forgetting what is behind and straining toward what is ahead, I press on toward the goal to win the prize for which God called me heavenward in Christ Jesus" (Philippians 3:13, 14).

In this verse, the phrase "forgetting what is behind" is translated from the Greek word *epilanthanomai*, which means "to forget or neglect." This does not mean to lose your memory about something, but to remove obstacles that might prevent the believer from running the race of the Christian life. Although others may have sinned against you and left you with the effects of that sin, God wants you to take the responsibility for dealing with whatever obstacles are in your life, no matter how they got there.

List any obstacles in your life that are interfering with your ability to live and grow in your Christian faith:

Identity as a Female

You may be afraid to deal with the obstacles in your life. You are not alone. God promises that He is beside you on the journey and will provide you with what you need to make it (Deuteronomy 31:6; Joshua 1:5; Hebrews 13:5).

"'For I know the plans I have for you,' declares the Lord, 'plans to prosper you and not to harm you, plans to give you hope and a future'" (Jeremiah 29:11).

Day 4

Another way that the image of God is tarnished is the emphasis that is sometimes placed on a young woman's outward, physical appearance. There is an undue influence in our society today which sends the wrong message about the standard of physical beauty. Along with the pressure to "fit in" with friends is the pressure to "look good" to others. You may feel pressure to stay below a certain weight or to wear a specific clothing size. You may be dissatisfied with your body shape or the way you look. This kind of pressure, combined with the desire to achieve perfection, can lead to an eating disorder. This section is going to focus on understanding what eating disorders are, and what can be done to help.

The Temple–Body Image

Consider this: the average woman today is 5'4" and weighs 142 lbs, while the average female model is 5'10" and weighs 112 lbs. Magazine and television advertisements portray primarily thin, beautiful, smiling models. The message often sent and received is that if you are thin you will be happy, successful, and liked by others. The problem is, this unrealistic message can lead to girls and young women believing that their happiness and popularity depend on achieving a certain dress size or weight. If unchecked, such a belief can develop into an eating disorder.

How many times have you been on a diet to try to lose weight?

___ Once ___ A few times ___ Several times ___ Never

It is estimated that in the United States, 50% of girls have dieted by the time they reach fourth grade (age 9). By the age of 17, 89% of young women have dieted.[5] For female athletes in particular, there are many pressures to stay thin. Although you don't have to be an athlete to diet, there are a few sports in particular that place athletes at risk for developing an eating disorder. Gymnastics, distance running, ballet, cross-country skiing, and figure skating tend to have a larger percentage of athletes develop disordered eating patterns.[6] An athlete may feel pressure to meet weight restrictions or look more attractive to judges. Athletes may even believe that a lower body fat will enhance their performance and give them an "edge" over the competition (this belief is not supported by research). The athletes most at risk for developing an eating disorder are often those who are particularly anxious and critical of their own athletic performance and who express these concerns by dissatisfaction with their bodies.[6]

As human beings, our desire for food is innate. Food provides our bodies with nutrients we need to function, grow, and develop. Food is also to be eaten for our enjoyment. The taste buds on our tongues allow us to enjoy the many different flavors of food. If a woman focuses on her weight, appearance, or body fat percentage, she may become obsessed with food. She may constantly think about what she is going to eat next, how many calories or fat grams she is eating, or how she can burn off calories she has consumed. This extreme focus on weight and food may indicate that the person has an eating disorder.

Read the following verses and write what God tells you about your body, food, and eating.
    Romans 6:13

    Romans 12:1, 2

    1 Corinthians 6:19, 20

    Proverbs 23:20, 21

    Matthew 6:25-27

    Philippians 3:17-21

Eating Disorders
Chances are, you have heard about eating disorders already. Most schools are doing more to educate students about eating disorders and how to get help if you are suffering from one.

There are two primary types of eating disorders: anorexia nervosa and bulimia. Anorexia results when people intentionally starve themselves by restricting the amount of food they eat, sometimes using excessive exercise to burn off fat. They are usually afraid of gaining any weight and may weigh themselves often. These people also believe that they are overweight even though they may be extremely thin.

Some of the other signs of anorexia include:

*an excessive weight loss in a fairly short period of time
*hair loss
*dry and brittle skin and nails
*the growth of fine body hair
*loss of muscle and body fat
*fainting spells
*loss of monthly menstrual period (amenorrhea)
*shortness of breath
*constipation
*refusal to eat or only eating very small amounts of food
*heart tremors
*depression
*an obsession with exercise

Bulimia also involves an obsession with food but may be difficult to detect. Individuals with bulimia eat large amounts of food at one time (binging), and then try to get rid of the calories by making themselves vomit, using laxatives, diuretics or enemas, or exercising. These methods of getting rid of food are called purging. People with bulimia usually binge and purge in secret, from once or twice a week to several times a day. The person can usually maintain a normal or slightly above normal body weight, which makes it difficult for others to tell that there is a problem. Signs of bulimia can include:

> *going to the bathroom for long periods of time to induce vomiting
> *binge eating without any noticeable weight gain
> *obsession with exercise
> *loss of monthly menstrual periods
> *dry, flaky skin
> *weakness and exhaustion
> *stomach pain
> *frequent sore throats
> *loss of tooth enamel leading to tooth decay
> *mood swings
> *use of drugs and alcohol

Another type of eating disorder that is similar to bulimia but does not involve purging is binge eating disorder. It involves eating large amounts of food at one time. The person might exercise excessively to try and burn off calories, but usually does not vomit or use laxatives. The person may also show signs of depression and/or drug and alcohol abuse.

TIME OUT!
Do you struggle with any of the symptoms mentioned? Which one(s)?

Remember, only a professional can actually diagnose someone with an eating disorder. Struggling with symptoms does not mean that you have an eating disorder, but it could indicate that you have some disordered thinking about food, your weight, or appearance. This might be an area for you to study further, or go to someone for help.

What causes an eating disorder?
Eating disorders are very complicated. Although there isn't one particular answer to this question, there are some common characteristics usually found in people who have an eating disorder. Typically, eating disorders are not really about food. Most often the issue is control. Individuals who are perfectionistic, compliant, experience low self-esteem and feelings of helplessness control their food and weight to manage stress or anxiety. Other factors may be present also, such as abuse, family problems, social rejection, or a critical or controlling parent.

What are the effects?
It is estimated that 5% of young women have either bulimia or anorexia.[3] Eating disorders are very serious problems because they can result in long-term physical damage to the individual and may even result in death. Anorexia can result in bone mineral loss leading to osteoporosis, low body temperature, low blood pressure, slowed metabolism and reflexes, irregular heartbeat, shrinkage of internal organs, and cardiac arrest. Bulimia can lead to dehydration, damage to internal organs such as bowels, liver, and kidneys, irregular heartbeat, and possibly heart attack. Binge eating disorder may result in high blood pressure, high cholesterol, gall bladder disease, diabetes, heart disease, and certain types of cancer.

For female athletes, eating disorders may result in symptoms which interfere with athletic performance, such as fatigue, weakness, leg cramps, and irregular heart rate. These symptoms are due to complications of eating disorders in the body such as low thyroid hormones, poor heart and circulatory function, and electrolyte imbalance. Amenorrhea (when the menstrual cycle stops) or irregular menses in female athletes should be taken seriously and checked out by a physician. These types of problems have been associated with osteoporosis (brittle bones) and infertility (inability to have children). Evidence also shows that crash dieting can make you more prone to injury. The United States Olympic Committee states that weight loss is only beneficial to an athlete if "the weight goal and rate of weight loss are realistic and the diet is balanced."[3]

What to do if you have an eating disorder
An eating disorder can put a woman in bondage. While she may start out feeling like she is in control of what she eats, eventually the eating disorder takes control and she finds herself enslaved to it. God's desire is that we not have anything in our lives that takes precedence over Him, including an eating disorder! John 8:36 says, "*If the Son sets you free, you will be free indeed.*" Jesus desires to set you free from the bondages of sin.

If you think that you or someone you know may be suffering from an eating disorder, get help. Some athletes may not want to get help because they are afraid they will be required to stop their sport. Usually athletes can continue training and competing while they are in treatment for the eating disorder, although in extreme cases, hospitalization may be necessary. When you go for help, teammates and friends don't necessarily have to know about the problem unless you want them to.

*Tell an adult you trust, such as a parent, coach, trainer, youth pastor, counselor, or physician.
*Learn about proper nutrition.
*If you need to lose weight, do so under the supervision of a nutritionist or physician.
*Accept professional help to learn more about yourself and your feelings to help you regain perspective and balance about food and your body.

If you, your doctor, and your coach agree that it is in your best interest to lose weight, make sure you do it in a safe way.

Review your current eating patterns. Talk with a doctor, nurse, or nutritionist to make sure that you are eating balanced meals that provide your body with the energy it needs.

Set a goal for yourself that includes the number of pounds you want to lose as well as the rate of loss. Weight loss should not be more than 2 pounds per week. Remember that muscle weighs more than fat. It is possible to lose fat pounds but not reduce weight if you are also increasing your muscle mass. A good way to assess this is by having your body fat percentage tested. The average female has 20-22% body fat.

Have your coach or athletic trainer weigh you on a regular basis to help monitor your progress. Keep in mind that a female's body retains water during her period, so you may notice a slight weight increase around that time of the month.[5, 6, 7]

Identity as a Female

Day 5

The Father Heart of God

There are many things in which you can place your identity, things that are temporary or based on what others value. Athletic ability, physical beauty, intelligence, and money are all things that the world values and many people admire. Sometimes you can tell where people place their identity based on how they introduce themselves to other people: "I'm an all-conference player"; "I was homecoming queen"; and "I'm a straight-A student" are all ways by which people identify their achievements and talents to others. Accomplishments such as these are admirable, but they don't make you any more valuable to God.

If God does not value us based on appearance or accomplishments, what does He value? In the first chapter of this book, we examined your identity as a Christian. Sometimes the admiration we receive from others is based on what we do or how we look. But not with God. He accepts you just as you are! He values you as a person, and part of who you are is your "femaleness." God values you as a female!

Read the following verses, and then fill in each statement with the missing word(s) that describe your identity:
Because of Christ...

I am like _____ for everyone on earth (Matthew 5:13)

I am like _____ for the whole world (Matthew 5:14)

I am a _____ of God (John 1:12)

My body is God's _____ (1 Corinthians 3:16)

I am a part of the _____ of Christ (1 Corinthians 12:27)

I am Christ's _____ (John 15:15)

I am a _____ sent out to tell everybody about Jesus (Acts 1:8)

I am a _____ and a _____ in this world (1 Peter 2:11)

I am _____, part of a _____ _____, a _____ to God (1 Peter 2:9)

One way to understand how we are to think of ourselves as women is to look at how Jesus treated women and what He said about them. In Jesus' day, women were treated more as property than as human beings. According to Jewish law, a man could divorce his wife for something as trivial as burning dinner, but a woman could not divorce her husband for any reason. Women were not allowed to testify in court because it was believed that a woman's opinion was worthless and women were not to be believed. Nobody was allowed to have contact with a woman during her menstrual cycle because she was "unclean," according to Jewish law. (Could you imagine if no one was allowed to have any contact with you during the time you had your period?) In Judaism, women were not allowed to learn from the Torah and and generally were not allowed to be in close association with men, including as a disciple.[8]

Jesus broke many cultural barriers with His treatment of women. He spent time teaching them, healing them (Matthew 26:7;

Mark 7:25; Luke 13:12), using them as examples in his teachings, and women were the first witnesses to the resurrection (Matthew 28:1-10; Mark 16:1-9; Luke 24:1-12).

Dorothy Sayers sums up the impact of Jesus' attitude toward and treatment of women:
> "Perhaps it is no wonder that the women were first at the Cradle and last at the Cross. They had never known a man like this Man–there never has been such another. A prophet and teacher who never nagged at them, never flattered or coaxed or patronized; who never made arch jokes about them, never treated them as 'The women, God help us!' or 'The ladies, God bless them!'; who rebuked without querulousness and praised without condescension; who took their questions and arguments seriously; who never mapped out their sphere for them, never urged them to be feminine or jeered at them for being female; who had no axe to grind and no uneasy male dignity to defend; who took them as he found them and was completely unself-conscious."[9]

You Go, Girl!

As a Christian, there are three foundational truths[10] you can believe in when it comes to your identity as a female and your relationship with God. Read the following verses and write out how they support each statement.

1. You are **accepted**.

> John 1:12

John 15:15

1 Corinthians 6:19-20

Ephesians 1:5

Colossians 1:14

2. You are **secure**.

John 10:28

Romans 8:1-2

Romans 8:35-39

Philippians 3:20

1 John 5:18

3. You are **significant**.

Matthew 5:13-14

John 15:16

Acts 1:8

1 Corinthians 3:16

Ephesians 2:10

Identity as a Female

Our prayer is that you continue to grow in your relationship with Christ as you develop your identity as a female Christian athlete.

Other Resources

Eating Disorders:
American Anorexia and Bulimia Association
201-836-1800

Remuda Ranch
One East Apache St.
Wickenburg, AZ 85390
1-800-445-1900

International Center for Sports Nutrition
502 South 44th Street, Rm. 3012
Omaha, NE 68105-1065
402-559-5505

3

Identity as an Athlete

We have examined your identity as a Christian and as a female. As an athlete, you have another special identity. You discipline yourself and make sacrifices to compete in your sport. Friends may identify you as a member of the volleyball or soccer team when they introduce you to others. It is easy to get wrapped up in your identity as an athlete, especially since society puts athletes up on a pedestal. Although there are many benefits to being an athlete, problems can also result. This chapter is going to focus on understanding who you are as an athlete.

Day 1
She's Got Game
In a popular 1998 television commercial, the Houston Comets' Cynthia Cooper is watching two men play a game of one-on-one basketball. After one of the men scores a basket, Cooper says, "You play like a girl." When the man recognizes the 1997 and 1998 Women's National Basketball Association (WNBA) Most Valuable Player, he smiles and says, "Thanks."

Female athletes are often stereotyped in a negative way. Have you ever been labeled because you were an athlete? What were some of the labels or stereotypes you've heard?

It used to be that when someone made a comment such as "you throw like a girl" or "you play like a girl," it was a put-down. For many years (and still today) young women would practice their sport against young men in an effort to improve their skills, their game, and because they hoped to hear the compliment "you play like a guy." As we approach the 21st century, young female athletes are fortunate to have many solid female role models to look up to. If you're a female, does it mean that you must only look up to and pattern yourself after other female athletes? No, but it is important to keep in mind that although athletic skills and abilities can be admired no matter what the gender of who has those abilities, they cannot always be imitated.

For example, Michael Jordan is respected and admired around the world for his basketball skills. Yet few, if any, women **or** men have the kind of physical and athletic talent that Jordan has. Does that prevent people from dreaming of being as good as Michael Jordan? No! The reality is, however, that overall there are physical differences between individuals that may result in differences in certain skills. God made you with the particular body shape, skills, and abilities you have. As an athlete, the goal is to develop your skills and abilities within the limitations you have as a human being. It does not mean that you are any less of an athlete because you do not have a 36-inch vertical jump or cannot hit over 60 home runs in a season. What counts is what you do with what you have.

Young women today have more female role models in college and professional sports than at any other time in history. It wasn't long ago, however, that girls were discouraged from participating in sports because athletic competition and physical activ-

Identity as an Athlete

ity were considered "unladylike" and potentially harmful because of the stress and strain on the female body. Now there are commercials of women pumping iron and gasping for breath as they push themselves to physical limits, looking very strong and athletic. Some people argue that female athletes are less feminine. These types of comments can stigmatize women who happen to be gifted athletically. It is also wrong to assume that if a woman is an athlete, she cannot be feminine at the same time. Where does that belief come from? Has the attention to athletics and competition changed the definition of what it means to be feminine? Some people argue that sports such as basketball, softball, and ice hockey have masculinized women. Others argue that you can be feminine regardless of what type of sport you play or how "rough" the game might be. Who is right?

Based on what you learned in the last chapter, write down what you think the word "feminine" means:

Do you think that being feminine takes away from your ability to compete as an athlete? Why or why not?

Madeline Manning Mims, four-time Olympian in track and field, explains it like this: "The problem in women's sports is that some women try to get their identity as athletes by taking on and focusing on the masculine characteristics. They buy into a lie that says being masculine makes them better athletes....God created me as a woman and He created me as an athlete. As an athlete, I can be aggressive. I can become the best in the world at my sport, but I can also choose to be a lady. It's a misconception that you can't be both feminine and athletic at the same time."[1]

The positive characteristics and qualities that young women develop through athletics can carry over into other areas of life. Discipline, self-control, confidence, and teamwork empower young women to take risks and challenge themselves in the classroom and the workplace.

Author Karen Drollinger talks about femininity and sports this way: "Femininity may not help a female athlete shoot free throws better, but accepting and fulfilling one's godly image gives her inner confidence to perform to the best of her ability. In other words, femininity is a necessity if women athletes are to be all that God created them to be."[2]

Femininity is about how you feel on the *inside* about being a female (your attitude) and how you demonstrate that attitude to others (your actions or behavior). Some female athletes confuse the desire to be a competitive athlete with the need to be masculine. Psalm 139 describes how God thinks about each of us and the way He made us, whether male or female. Read Psalm 139 and write below what the verses say about you:

I am _____ (v. 1)

I am _____ (v. 5)

I am _____ (v. 10)

I am _____ (v. 14)

Identity as an Athlete

The truth is, God values you as a female! You are His creation. Remember the discussion on what it means to be in the image of God? God transcends gender. God is described using both masculine and feminine characteristics. This does not mean that we need to start referring to God as "Mother," but as females created in the image of God, our gender somehow reflects that part of the divine image. It is important to consider how we reflect that uniqueness of ourselves to others.

Most female athletes like to dress in athletic gear such as t-shirts, gym shorts, sweatshirts, and sweatsuits. After all, such clothing is part of the job, and very comfortable for everyday wear! However, it is possible that if sweatshirts and gym shorts are what you wear the majority of the time, it may be more of a reflection about what you believe about yourself or how you want others to perceive you. There is nothing wrong with wearing sweatshirts. But is wearing this type of clothing on a regular basis a way of covering up your insecurity about your femininity? This is a difficult question. If your attitude about yourself is demonstrated in part by your behavior, then that would include what you choose to wear. Here are some questions to think about that might give you some insight:

How do you respond when others compliment you on your appearance? Do you feel good about yourself, or doubt what they say?

How do you feel when you wear dresses or clothing that is clearly feminine? Do you feel confident or uncomfortable?

Some females identify so much as an athlete that they ignore their femininity. This does not mean that you have to wear a dress and heels every day. It does mean taking time to consider what image you are presenting to others off the court. Besides the wardrobe you choose, it is just as important to consider your speech, attitude, and how you relate to others.

How can you develop your feminine qualities the way God intended? Here are some suggestions:

1. Get to know the One who created you as a female. Spend time in God's word finding out what He says about you as a human being created in His image.

2. Develop the feminine qualities and characteristics in yourself that will show others that you are confident as a female both on and off the court. Examine the areas of your life to see what message you are sending to others in your dress, language (gossip, using profanity), relationships, etc.

3. Spend time with an older, godly woman that you respect and discuss with her the issue of femininity and athletics. It is sometimes helpful to receive direction from others who can relate to problems or questions that you are having.

Day 2
The Competitive Female
The world tells us that second place is not good enough. You have to be Number One to really be successful. How many commercials have you seen where the spokesperson is the

Identity as an Athlete 79

runner-up? These messages can develop a win-at-all-cost mentality that results in deep disappointment if the goal isn't achieved. It also sends the wrong message about what it means to be competitive.

One of the common characteristics of successful athletes is that they tend to be *competitive*. Competitiveness can be viewed as a negative trait. Comments such as "she always has to win" and "she always keeps score–nothing is just for fun" often describe an individual who defines competitiveness and success with one word: winning. As an athlete, success can not mean that winning is the only goal or you may begin to judge yourself and your team by your win-loss record.

Have you ever prepared for a game with the attitude "The other team is much better than us, and we'll never be able to beat them. We might as well just practice what it's going to feel like to lose the game. There's no way we can win." Hopefully not! If you ever did, chances are you did lose the game. A competitive athlete is willing to take on the challenge of pushing herself to improve the abilities and skills she possesses in an effort to defeat an opponent. Competitiveness is desiring to improve as an athlete and to perform your best in every situation.

What does the Bible say about competitiveness? (Read 1 Corinthians 9:24-27)

When you are competing as an athlete, it is natural to want to beat the player or team you are competing against. But what happens when the opponent is a friend or a teammate? In individual sports you may have to play against a friend. In team sports, you may find yourself competing against a friend for the starting spot. Can you stay friends and be competitive at the same time? Think about an experience when you had to compete against a friend. How did you handle it? Did competing against each other affect your friendship? If so, how?

Consider Stephanie and Alicia, two young women who had been friends since grade school. Both were setters on their high school volleyball team, and they attended the same church and participated in youth group together. Although Stephanie was a good volleyball player, Alicia had more athletic talent and was chosen as the starting setter for the team.

At first, Stephanie acted as though she didn't care. After the first few games, however, she began to resent the attention that Alicia got from the coach and other players. Soon, Stephanie did not want anything to do with Alicia. She even considered attending youth group at a different church so she wouldn't have to see her. These two friends were suddenly not speaking to each other. It was even worse at practices, when the two were expected to run drills with each other. Stephanie began to dislike Alicia more and more. At times Stephanie even found herself wishing that Alicia would play poorly or have an injury so that she could take over her spot as starter. Soon, Stephanie was more concerned about how she practiced and played compared to Alicia than whether the team won or lost.

This scenario often happens among teammates. What starts out as healthy competition can result in jealousy, envy, and resent-

Identity as an Athlete

ment. Read the following verses and write down some of the potential results of jealousy.

James 3:14

Proverbs 14:30

Envy is a feeling of discontent and ill will because of another person's advantages, abilities, possessions, etc. Envy results when your focus moves from what you have or are able to do to what another person has or is able to do. In the situation just mentioned, Stephanie stopped focusing on her own abilities and began to feel jealous that Alicia was starting instead of her. Rather than talking to Alicia or the coach about her feelings, Stephanie began to pull away from her friendship with Alicia. As a result, the envy she felt continued to grow into resentment.

Where does envy come from?

Galatians 5:19-21

1 Corinthians 3:3

Ecclesiastes 4:4

How does Scripture tell us to handle jealousy and envy?

Galatians 5:26

1 Corinthians 13:4

1 Peter 2:1-3

1 John 1:9

Matthew 5:23

Whom are You Playing For?
When an athlete becomes too focused on her athletic performance, she can begin to base her identity and worth as a person on how she performs as an athlete. There is a fine line between developing confidence as an athlete and basing your identity on how you play.

Whom do you try to please with your performance as an athlete? Teammates? Coaches? Parents? Fans? The Bible says that we are to practice and play in the game as if God is the only one watching us. We have an audience of one. *"Whatever you do, work at it with all your heart, as working for the Lord, not for [people]"* (Colossians 3:23). Some Christian athletes are able to keep their focus on the Lord during competition by mentally reminding themselves whom they are playing for. They might pick an open seat in the bleachers and imagine that Jesus is sitting there

Identity as an Athlete

watching them. Each time they look at that spot, they are reminded of whom they are really playing for.

Competition can be a positive thing. It can drive us to work harder, practice more, to be better than we ever thought possible. It can also become the most important thing. As an athlete you practice and train to be your best. However, you can cross the line to where winning becomes the most important thing. You may even start to base your worth as an athlete or a person on how you play!

Betsy King, a professional golfer and a member of the Ladies Professional Golf Association (LPGA) Hall of Fame, said this about the pressures of athletic competition: "As a Christian I can relax. Whatever happens, I still have God and eternity. I'm not basing my self-worth on my success as golfer."[1] Betsy King understands that to excel in athletics, it is necessary to have a competitive drive to keep you practicing and desiring to improve. However, if your worth as a person is based on how successful you are as an athlete, there will be times when you will probably find yourself riding an emotional roller-coaster. As a Christian, you are guaranteed eternal life based on your relationship with Christ, not on how many points you score or how many runs you bat in. Your worth as a person is already established, and nothing in your athletic performance can change that!

Day 3
Obstacles Female Athletes Face
There are several types of obstacles that can interfere with an athlete's desire to compete and glorify God. At the same time,

those same obstacles that might trip you up and cause you to stumble can also be used to glorify God. This section will look at a few of the most common obstacles female athletes face.

Remember that as females, we are gifted with an ability to relate emotionally to other people. At times, we may also relate emotionally to situations. Competition can draw out emotions that are counterproductive to your performance and possibly damaging to a friendship.

Jenny played forward on her school's soccer team. She was a good-natured player who had been voted the "spirit award" by her teammates the year before. During a game against a rival school, Jenny was tripped by one of the opposing players. The referee did not see it, and the opposing player continued to taunt Jenny during the game. Jenny began to fume. After the other player tried several times to trip her again, Jenny felt her blood boil. She was so angry, she wanted to get back at the other player somehow.

How would you respond in this situation if you were Jenny?

Remember that as a Christian, you are a witness at **all** times, even during a game. Your actions (or reactions) may have a big influence on others. During athletic competition there are almost always situations in which one athlete or team feels that officials did not make the right call, or the other team is playing unfairly. How you respond in these situations will reveal how much control Christ has over you.

Identity as an Athlete

Even though it may be tempting to taunt opponents or "trash talk," the Bible clearly states that we are not to try and provoke anger in others (Proverbs 15:1; 30:33). In the same way, we are to have control over ourselves and our emotions so that we do not retaliate when someone offends us (Proverbs 29:11). Read the following verses and write down in your own words what they say about your behavior during competition:

Colossians 3:8

Romans 12:19, 20

Ecclesiastes 7:9

1 Peter 3:9

Drugs and Alcohol
It is amazing how many athletes will sacrifice hours of time to practice, stay in shape, and fine-tune their athletic skills without realizing that in their spare time they are doing great damage to their bodies and their athletic potential. It is estimated that 63% of students graduating from high school in the United States have been drunk at some point. In addition, 22% report that they smoke cigarettes daily; 21% currently smoke marijuana; and 17% have used inhalants.[3] Drug and alcohol use is often a factor in teenage automobile accidents, suicides, homicides, increased sexual activity, and sexual assaults.

We are told that our bodies are temples of the Lord, a living sacrifice to Him (1 Corinthians 6:19-20). We are to treat our bodies as if they don't belong to us anymore, but to God! Can you imagine what your mom or dad would do if they showed up at home and found that there were a bunch of people partying and drinking, tearing apart the house without caring what damage they did? In a sense, that is how you are treating God if you are damaging His temple (your body) by abusing drugs and alcohol. Does He still care for you? Yes, but you are making it difficult for Him to "clean house" by the decisions you are making.

Consider the following questions to see if you might have a problem with drugs or alcohol:

____ You can't predict whether or not you will use drugs or get drunk.

____ You believe that in order to have fun you need to drink and/or use drugs.

____ You turn to alcohol and/or drugs after a confrontation or argument, or to relieve uncomfortable feelings.

____You drink more or use more drugs to get the same effect that you once got with smaller amounts.

____ You drink and/or use drugs alone.

____ You remember how last night began, but not how it ended, so you're worried you may have a problem.

____ You have trouble at work or in school because of your drinking or drug use.

____You make promises to yourself or others that you'll stop getting drunk or using drugs.

____ You feel alone, scared, miserable, and depressed.

If any of these statements describe you, it may be an indication that you have a problem with drugs or alcohol. You need to get help. Talk with a parent, coach or another adult that you trust. (The Fellowship of Christian Athletes [FCA] also has a program called "One Way 2 Play–Drug Free," which emphasizes making a commitment to stay away from drugs and alcohol using faith in Jesus Christ and accountability with others to help keep the commitment. You can get information about this program from an FCA staff member in your area or from the National FCA office by calling 1-800-289-0909.)

If you attend parties where alcohol and drugs are used, you may not only be tempted to participate, but others may question your faith. Romans 14:20-21 tells us, "*Do not destroy the work of God for the sake of food [or alcohol]. All food is clean, but it is wrong for a [person] to eat anything that causes someone else to stumble. It is better not to eat meat or drink wine or to do anything else that will cause your brother to fall.*" You have a responsibility as a representative of Christ to live your life so that others see something different.

Injuries
One of the difficult challenges of any athlete's career is battling injuries. It can be frustrating to spend hours of off-season conditioning and training only to be hampered during the season by a nagging injury, or kept from playing at all because of necessary surgery or rehabilitation. Most athletes, at some point in their career, will experience some type of injury. It may not be serious enough to keep you out of competition, but it may slow you down or make you uncomfortable for awhile. As Christians, we are told in Romans 8:28, "*We know that in all things God works for the good of those who love him, who have been called according to his*

purpose." This includes injuries. Even though it may be hard to see at the time, God can and wants to use your injury in some way to glorify Himself and to draw you closer to Him.

Have you ever been injured? What did you learn through it?

Read the following verses and write out how God intends to use suffering in the lives of His children, and what He desires your response to be.

James 1:2-4

>   Your response:

>   How God can use it:

Hebrews 12:5-11

>   Your response:

>   How God can use it:

1 Peter 1:6-7

>   Your response:

How God can use it:

2 Corinthians 4:7-11

Your response:

How God can use it:

Make no mistake, God loves you and cares for you. Often an injury puts you at a crossroads of faith. Do you complain and stay angry because of what has happened, or trust in God's will? Keep in mind that if you are following Him and living according to His Word, then nothing can happen to you without God allowing it. Sometimes suffering an injury will develop qualities and characteristics in us that were not there before. Read Romans 5:3-5 and write out the qualities that can develop out of suffering:

Pressure

Have you ever been in a situation where the outcome of the game depended on you? It can be an intimidating experience. All eyes are focused on you, and suddenly your mouth gets dry. Your palms start sweating, and you notice that your heart is beating about 100 times faster than normal. Your legs feel like rubber as you step up to the plate in the seventh inning with the bases loaded, two outs, and your team behind by one run. Or it is the final set of the match and all you have to do is get the serve in bounds. Or you're at the free throw line with a chance to send the game into overtime. Suddenly, you hear the screaming of fans, and you realize they are all depending on you. You have trouble concentrating and wonder what the coach will say if you blow it.

It can be difficult to maintain a sense of calm in this type of situation. What you are focusing on will help determine the outcome. The more you focus on the situation, you will probably start to feel overwhelmed. A certain level of anxiety is usually common in most athletes, but too much anxiety can interfere with your ability to perform. God desires that we not allow fear and anxiety to interfere with what He has called us to do. Read the following verses and write out what God says about anxiety.

Isaiah 41:10

1 Peter 5:7

2 Timothy 1:7

As Christians, we know that there is nothing in life that we need to be worried or anxious about, because regardless of the outcome, our relationship with God is secure. He loves us and values us regardless of our athletic performance. If you begin to experience anxiety, follow these suggestions to help yourself refocus on the task at hand.

1. Visualize yourself successfully performing the task. Close your eyes and "see" yourself going through your routine and making the free throws, or swinging and connecting with the ball. This is something you can also develop during practice.

2. Focus your thoughts. Rather than listening to the crowd or teammates, have one or two particular thoughts that you focus on. It could be a Scripture or even a single word. Focusing your thoughts will help to block out distracting noise.

3. Relax. It is difficult to do almost anything when you are tense. Take deep breaths and stretch if you need to. Remember that you have probably done this activity a thousand times before, and this time is not that much different.

4. Keep it in perspective. You can't evaluate your performance as an athlete on one moment or situation in a game. When your identity is in Christ, you are assured of your worth and value regardless of how you perform.

Day 4
The Confidence Factor
What does it mean to be confident?
Webster's Dictionary defines confidence as "To be assured, certain of oneself." Confidence is a "firm belief; trust; reliance; belief in one's own abilities." These definitions focus on confidence based on one's own abilities.

How can you tell if people are confident in themselves?

As Christians, we are to have a different type of confidence. Read the following verses and jot down where they say we should place our confidence:

2 Corinthians 5:6-9

Philippians 1:6

1 John 5:13, 14

Confidence Under Pressure
The Hope College women's basketball team won the NCAA Division III Championship in 1990. During the game, Hope fell behind by 20 points with 10 minutes left in the game. Many teams would have lost confidence at that point. However, the team continued to press on, and with five seconds left, a 3-point basket tied the game. In a last-second scramble for a loose ball, Dina Disney of Hope College was fouled. She went to the free throw line with only a few seconds left on the clock to decide a national championship and sank two free throws to win the game. Afterwards, when she was interviewed by reporters, Dina was asked how she stayed calm under the pressure. Dina replied, "While I was standing there I just kept repeating to myself Philippians 4:13, '*I can do all things through Christ who strengthens me.*'" Dina's focus was in the right place. She was not thinking of the screaming fans or the pressure of the situation. Her confidence was in the Lord, and by reminding herself she stayed calm

Identity as an Athlete

and was able to make the free throws.

Confidence Gone Overboard
Remember the definitions of confidence that dealt with believing in oneself and one's own abilities? This type of confidence can go too far and develop into arrogance. Arrogance is the belief that you are better than or superior to others. An arrogant person often puts herself up on a pedestal.

Have you ever known someone who was arrogant?

How did he/she show that he/she was arrogant?

Even if you are the best player on your team or one of the best players in your sport, you are still accountable for how you treat others. The Bible is clear about what our response is to be when we are more talented than others.

> Philippians 2:3-8

> Proverbs 15:33

> 1 Peter 5:5-7

Out of the Slumps
It is rare to find a team or athlete at any level that finishes a season undefeated. Most athletes know the feeling of not only los-

ing, but sometimes an athlete or a team has a period of not playing well, also known as a "slump."

Remember a time when you were in a slump as an athlete. What did you think about yourself as an athlete during that time?

When an athlete is in a slump, she may focus on the fact that she is not playing well, or wonder what others think of her performance. Her confidence may start to decrease, and she may experience frustrations in other areas of her life. A slump is a trial. It is a time of testing that will reveal what is really on the inside. Read the following verses and write out what God says about experiencing a slump:

2 Corinthians 4:7-9

Philippians 3:13, 14

Day 5

More than an Athlete: Finding the Balance
Talk to most parents about the activities of their kids and this is what you may hear from a lot of parents: "Well, Monday we have soccer practice and Girl Scouts. Tuesday is Little League night, and Wednesday is soccer games and then youth group. Thursday is a night off, but then Friday and Saturday are usually full of tournaments and practices." It's no wonder many kids (and adults) don't have fun when they participate in athletics. It's too much like work! There is a trend in our society for young

Identity as an Athlete

athletes to "specialize," to focus on developing their skills and abilities in one particular sport at an early age. Summer camps, specialty camps, private coaches, and youth leagues all emphasize the development of the physical and athletic talent a young woman might have. But what about the rest of her? Let's take a look at where your time is spent during a typical week. Fill in the pie graph on this page, dividing the sections into the following areas: school, family, friends, work, athletics, and God. Each section of the graph should represent the average amount of time you spend in that area during the week.

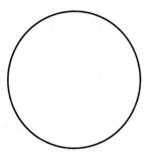

What area of your life do you spend the most amount of time on?

The least amount of time?

You can tell what is a priority in someone's life by the amount of time they spend on it. The difficulty in athletics is that we often put so much time into it that pretty soon we don't have time for anything else. You can lose focus on what is most important. Read Luke 10:38-42. Have you ever felt like Martha? Working hard to please God, feeling like you're carrying most of the load when others don't help in the way you want them to? Read verses 40 and 41 again and write down three words that describe Martha as she focused on doing:

(v. 40) _____

(v. 41) _____

(v. 41) _____

Jesus said that Mary had chosen the only thing that was needed, and it was better than what Martha had chosen. What was it that Mary had chosen?

My Peace I Give You
What do you think of when you hear the word "peace"?

In the Bible, peace can mean harmonious relationships between people or nations, freedom from war, and a harmonious relationship between God and people. It also is used to describe a sense of rest and contentment that is only found in a relationship with Jesus Christ.[4] In John 14:27, Jesus says to His disciples, "*Peace I leave with you; my peace I give you. I do not give to you as the world gives. Do not let your hearts be troubled and do not be afraid.*" Jesus is explaining to the disciples that total well-being and inner rest is found in fellowship with God. If you are looking for real rest and contentment, you don't have to look any further than Him.

Identity as an Athlete

Have you ever experienced the peace described in John 14? When?

When we feel restless and caught up with the worries of life, it is often an indication that we are looking for security and peace in the wrong places. If you lived every minute of every day with the kind of peace that we're talking about, what would be different about you?

4

Relationships as a Christian

This week we are going to take a look at how we relate with others from a Christian perspective. We will cover character issues, forgiveness, servanthood, how to love others, and how to share the Lord with others.

Day 1
Whom are You Hanging Around?
First, let's take a look at who you are.

Have you ever noticed that when you spend a lot of time with friends or teammates, you start to think alike, say the same phrases and expressions, and maybe even dress alike. You become like those you spend time with.

As an athletic teenager growing up in the Midwest, Kathy spent a lot of time with her teammates. They would have their own little jokes that no one else really understood because others had not "been there" to experience what they were talking about. Thinking back to her high school and college days, Kathy really doesn't remember too many specifics about the games she played. There are a few that stand out, like the time the team pulled off a triple play in the bottom of the seventh inning to win the game. Or the time they came from-behind to win a game in the conference tournament, which allowed them to qualify for Nationals. But what Kathy remembers most are the lifelong friendships that she made. Games come and go, but relationships are what really matter.

As you look at the study for today, you will notice that LIFE IS RELATIONSHIPS. It's what happens in your relationships that counts. You have been given a relationship with God, and that relationship will affect all of your other relationships.

Relationships exist in three dimensions:
    Your relationship to yourself,
    Your relationship to others,
    and Your relationship to God.

All three are closely connected. What you think of yourself will dramatically affect how you relate with God and with others. This is best seen in the quality of your relationships and how you handle different situations in your life.

Many factors influence and contribute to who you are. What you spend your time doing, what you listen to, what you watch (television, movies, etc.), what you read, who you spend time with, where you came from, and what you believe others think of you all play a role in how you view yourself.

Taking a Look Inside
List 3 things you like about yourself:

List 3 things you don't like about yourself:

Which list was easier to make? Many people find it easier to think about what they *don't* like about themselves. Why do we tend to dwell on the negative things? James Hufstetler says it this way:

> "You are the result of the attentive, careful, thoughtful, intimate, detailed, creative work of God. Your personality, your sex, your height, your features are what they are because God made them precisely that way. He made you the way He did because that is the way He wants you to be. If God had wanted you to be basically and creatively different He would have made you differently. Your genes and chromosomes and creaturely distinctives—even the shape of your nose and ears—are what they are by God's design."[1]

In his book *Trusting God*, Jerry Bridges tells us, "He [God] gave you the body, the mental abilities, and the basic personality you have because that is the way He wanted you to be. And He wanted you to be just that way because He loves you and wants to glorify Himself through you."[2]

Taking a Look at Jesus

How you view God and your relationship with Him will also affect how you relate with others. Describe what you know of Jesus' relationship to God.

Jesus modeled for us the type of relationship we are to have with God. Read the following verses, and write down what you notice about Jesus' relationship to the Father:

John 4:34

John 5:19, 20, 30

John 6:38

John 7:16

John 12:49

Jesus was totally dependent on the Father. Every move He made, every word He spoke, every thought He had showed His total dependence on God through the Holy Spirit. Step by step, Jesus was led into doing all the Father Himself did. The first step was dependence (admitting He could do nothing on His own), then obedience (doing what the Father did or said). For Jesus, the combination of dependence and obedience led to a deep closeness with the Father.

What does your relationship with the Lord look like? What things can you do to deepen your closeness with the Father?

Taking a Look at Others
Who you are is best shown through your actions. This is where your heart is revealed. It shows what is really inside.

Describe what you think Jesus is like. (Name some characteristics)

Compassionate, loving, servant, honest, trustworthy, reliable, kind. These may have been some of the first things that came to your mind. But did you also think of words like radical, full of joy, not afraid of confrontation, and bold? Have you ever noticed that wherever Jesus went others followed Him? He attracted people to Himself.

Who you are is also shown in how you relate to others. Think about your relationships. List one or two characteristics you would like to develop in your relationships.

Allow God to work on these areas of your life. Ask Him to show you what you need to do. Life is a process. None of us are perfect. We are learning and we are growing into the character and image of Christ.

Enduring Even When it Hurts
The greatest challenges often come in the heat of the battle. People will evaluate your character by what you say and by your actions not only in everyday life, but also during competition. It is said that when you are bumped (put in difficult situations), what is inside you spills out. This "spilling out" often shows up during athletic competition when you become frustrated or angry. These difficult circumstances, which all of us go through at different points in our lives, can be used to transform us into the image of Christ.

Read Proverbs 17:3 and Zechariah 13:9.

What does the Lord mean when He talks about refining us like silver and gold? This process of refining–separating the dross (impurities) from the pure gold or silver–happened when the metal was reduced to a liquid state by applying heat and solvents (medicine).

This is what happens: a goldsmith refiner never leaves her crucible once it is on the fire. The gold sits in a type of medicine. The medicine does its appointed work on the gold, then the fire heats it. Then the goldsmith lifts the gold out with a pair of tongs, lets it cool, rubs it between her fingers, and if not satisfied, puts it back again in fresh medicine. This time the goldsmith blows the fire hotter than it was before, and each time the gold is put into the crucible the fire is increased. The gold cannot stand the heat at first, but it can now. Too much heat would have destroyed it at first, but later actually helps it. The goldsmith knows the gold is purified when she can see her face reflected in the liquid gold. Only then is it pure.

The same is true of us. God will use circumstances (medicine and fire) to bring the imperfections of our lives to the surface. He does this until He can see His reflection in us.

Read Romans 8:29 and 2 Corinthians 3:18. Why does the Lord refine us?

God wants to change us into the image of His Son. He uses relationships and circumstances to accomplish this very thing. One of God's goals is to build your character, to make it look more like His character. Everything God does, He does to build your character and to develop your relationship with Him and with others. You will become like those you hang around. Do you want to be like Jesus? Hang around Him and others who have a relationship with Him!

Day 2
Injuries that Heal
Forgiveness
If you have ever been injured during practice or competition, then you know the feeling of physical pain. If you have ever been cut from a team or hurt by the remarks from a teammate or coach, then you know the feeling of emotional pain. Whether you have been injured or have caused an injury to someone else, the wounds are real and need to be healed.

As we saw in the previous section, who you are (your character) is shown by how you relate to others. One of the foundations of the Christian faith is FORGIVENESS. In our relationships, we must understand the importance of being able to give and receive forgiveness.

Write out what forgiveness means to you.

One definition of forgiveness: "an act of the will to give up resentment, grudges or the desire to punish the offender; willingness to release another from his accountability for wrong."

The following story illustrates how unforgiveness can drastically affect relationships.

Once there were two unmarried sisters who lived together, but because of an unresolved disagreement over an insignificant issue, they stopped speaking to each other. Since they were either unable or unwilling to move out of their small house, they continued to use the same rooms, eat at the same table, use the same appliances, and sleep in the same room together without talking to each other. A chalk line divided the sleeping area into two halves, separating doorways as well as the fireplace. Through the black of the night, each could hear the deep breathing of the other, but because both were unwilling to take the first step toward forgiving the silly offense, they coexisted for years in grinding silence.[3]

Now that's taking things to an extreme. But you can see how unforgiveness can and will affect your relationships.

Understanding Forgiveness
Write out 1 Peter 3:18.

Forgiveness comes as a result of Christ's death and brings us into a right relationship with God. In the book of Colossians, Paul was writing to people in the city of Colossae who had put their total trust in Jesus Christ.

"You were dead in sin and your sinful desires were not yet cut away. Then He gave you a share in the very life of Christ, for He forgave all your sins, and blotted out the charges proved against you, the list of His

commandments which you had not obeyed. He took this list of sin and destroyed it by nailing it to Christ's cross" (Colossians 2:13, 14, The Living Bible).

According to this verse, how many of your sins have been forgiven?

What has God done with your sin?

When the letter to the Colossians was written, "this list of sin" referred to an itemized note that was nailed to the cell door of a prisoner. This note listed every crime that the prisoner had committed. After the sentence was served for these crimes, those in authority removed the list and wrote "paid in full" on the paper. The prisoner used this as proof that he or she could never be tried again for those crimes. The believer who trusts Christ's payment for her sins can never be tried again. You have full forgiveness from God.

When you trust Christ for the forgiveness of your sins, all your sins are forgiven–past, present, and future. Look up these verses and write what they say about forgiveness:

Psalm 130:4

Acts 10:43

Ephesians 1:7; 4:32

Colossians 3:13

Receiving Forgiveness
The medical profession will tell you that pain is good because it warns you that something is wrong. When you place your hand on a hot stove, the pain signals you to take your hand off the stove before you do further damage. When we do something that is not pleasing to God, the Holy Spirit convicts us of sin, and we feel guilt. This guilt is good because it shows us that something is wrong and we need to do something about it.

Write out Ephesians 4:30.

Conviction is one role of the Holy Spirit. Conviction from the Holy Spirit is a specific feeling of guilt that can be related to a particular, precise act or attitude.

When the Holy Spirit brings a specific act or attitude to your mind that you know is not pleasing to Him, you must deal with it right away. Receiving forgiveness includes:

    1. Telling God that you have sinned.
    2. Accepting that God has forgiven you.
    3. Trusting God to change your attitude and actions.

Read 1 John 1:9 and write the verse below.

If you do not deal with sin when you are convicted, your fellowship with God will be hindered. A guilty conscience can affect your relationships with others, your emotions, and even your physical health. You will not experience God's peace and freedom, but instead will be filled with anxiety.

In his book *Healing for Damaged Emotions*, David Seamands writes, "So many Christians say, 'Yes, I know that God has forgiven me, but I can never forgive myself.'" This statement is a contradiction in terms. How can you believe that God has forgiven you, and then not forgive yourself? When God forgives, He buries your sins in the sea of His forgiveness and His forgetfulness. As Corrie ten Boom said, "He then puts a sign on the bank which says, 'NO FISHING ALLOWED.' You have no right to dredge up anything that God has forgiven and forgotten. He has put it behind His back. You can forgive yourself."[4]

Is there anything for which you need to ask forgiveness? Take some time to ask the Holy Spirit to bring to your mind any attitude or action which is displeasing to Him. If there is anything, He will show you. Remember that there is no guilt that the Lord cannot take care of. Your part is to draw near to Him.

Forgiving Others
Conflict between people is a normal and predictable part of any relationship. As you spend time with others, conflict will happen. The way you deal with this conflict will determine how healthy your relationships are. Without forgiveness, there is a breakdown in relationships. This breakdown can result in emotional conflict.

You may ask, "But what about the times when someone really hurts me, and what if it was totally intentional? Do I still have to forgive them?"

What kinds of "wounds" hurt you the most? Insults? Rejection? Physical abuse? Prejudice? What kind of wound is the most difficult for you to forgive?

One thing to keep in mind is that if you do not receive the forgiveness of God, you will find it almost impossible to forgive those who have deeply hurt you or who have failed you in some way. You must first receive God's forgiveness before you can extend it to someone who has hurt you.

Read Matthew 18:23-35.

Day 3
Playing with All Your Heart–Loving Others
What do you think of when you hear the word "love"?

A definition the world might use would be a gushy emotion or feeling for another. If someone is "in love," that person is probably saying they have a strong emotional attachment and desire for another. If later they don't have that strong emotional attachment, they say they have fallen "out of love." To the world, love is an emotion. You can love someone one minute and not the next.

God's Love Toward You
What does God say love is? Read 1 Corinthians 13:4-7 and write out God's definition of love.

Though God loves you, He is always holy and pure, and does not fluctuate according to moods or circumstances. The motive behind Jesus dying on the cross for our sins was His amazing and incredible love for each of us. God loves you with a mighty love that has no beginning and no end. He loves you as much today as He did two thousand years ago when He physically demonstrated His love for you through Christ.

In fact, God's love for each of us is far beyond our human understanding. When Paul prayed for the Christians in the church at Ephesus, he prayed *"that they may be able to comprehend with all the saints what is the breadth and length and height and depth, and to know the love of Christ which surpasses knowledge"* (Ephesians 3:18, 19a).

God's love is giving. Love in God's terms is an action. It is desiring the best for another and acting upon that desire to make it happen.

Read Romans 5:8 and write it below.

How did God demonstrate His love for us?

According to the following verses, briefly explain some of the ways God expresses His love to you:

Psalm 68:19

Romans 5:5

Ephesians 1:3

Colossians 1:12-14

Hebrews 12:6

Your Love Toward Others
Not only does God love with an everlasting love, but He also desires for you to have His love and to express His love. Read 1 John 4:11-12. Write out what John's greatest desire is for his fellow believers.

Jesus longs to pour out His love into your life and through your life to be a blessing to others. So how do you apply this to your life? How do you love with God's love? John 13:34 says, "*A new command I give you: Love one another. As I have loved you, so you must love one another.*" We should love others as Jesus loves us.

Let's take a look again at 1 Corinthians 13:4-7. Write out all the words that describe what love is:

Write out the words that describe what love is NOT:

Think of the people in your life (parents, siblings, teammates, classmates, teachers, coaches, etc). Are you motivated by love to be patient with them, kind to them, not envious of them, not

Relationships as a Christian

boastful around them, not rude to them, not seeking just your own interests when you are with them, and not easily angered at them?

TIME OUT!
It is always easier to show love to those who love us back. But Jesus said we are also to love those that we don't get along with. Think of someone that you find it hard to get along with. Write down at least one way that you will demonstrate Christ's love to this person.

Day 4
Practicing Your Serve–Being a Servant
When a player serves the ball in tennis or volleyball, that player takes the initiative to put the ball in play. As a servant, we take the initiative to minister and show Jesus' love and character to those around us.

During Lisa's senior year in college, she always helped get the equipment out each day at practice. One of the freshman on the team noticed and asked Lisa why she did it. She thought that since Lisa was a senior, she would be exempt from helping with such duties. Lisa, who was a Christian, could have taken the attitude that underclassmen do every little menial job, but she felt it was important for her team to work together even in this small area. She wanted to show by example that every job had significance, that she was a servant leader, and that every player was of great value to the team.

Mark 10:45 says, *"For even the Son of Man did not come to be served, but to serve, and to give his life a ransom for many."* Jesus came to serve. Since God is forming us into the image of His Son, it makes sense that God desires for us to serve. God is building into us the same servant qualities that characterized Jesus. What does this look like? Let's take a look at the life of Jesus. Chuck Swindoll, author of *Improving Your Serve*, once said that in all his study of Scripture he could only find one place where Jesus, in His own words, describes His "inner man." And when He described Himself, He used only two words. This description is found in Matthew 11:28-29.

What two words does Jesus use in verse 29 to describe Himself?

In case you didn't see it, Jesus says He is gentle and humble. "Gentle" means "strength under control." It is a word used to describe a wild stallion that has been tamed. "Humble in heart" means "lowly." It is a picture of a helper, but not someone who is weak or insignificant. It is the image of someone who is unselfish and thoughtful toward others.

Read John 13:3-17.

This is a scene at the last supper before Jesus was to be crucified. In Jesus' time, they did not have paved roads like we have today. And obviously they did not drive cars. They walked from place to place on dirt roads. And when it rained, they walked on muddy roads. In those days it was customary for a slave to wash the feet of those entering the house. If there was no slave, then one of the first to enter the house would usually do this job. List some observations about how Jesus showed His gentle and humble heart to His disciples based on what you read in John 13:3-17.

As we look at how Jesus showed His disciples to act (both outwardly and inwardly), we learn several things about being a servant. The following are insights from Charles Swindoll's book, *Improving Your Serve*.

Being a Servant is Unannounced

When Jesus rose and began washing the feet of His disciples, He did not broadcast what He was about to do. He also did not do it out of anger, thinking, "Well, no one else is going to do this, so I guess I have to." Jesus washed the disciples' feet to show them that they must serve one another and think of others before themselves.

Being a Servant Includes Receiving Graciously as Well as Giving Graciously

As you look at Peter's response to the Lord, he said, "No, you shall never wash my feet." And Jesus said, "Unless I wash you, you have no part with me!" On the surface, it sounds like a pretty harsh statement. But you must remember that a servant not only knows how to give but also how to receive. Both are very important!

Being a Servant is Not a Sign of Inner Weakness, but Incredible Strength

Some may think of servants as weak individuals, but nothing could be further from the truth. Jesus was emphatic when He told Peter that he would have no part with Jesus unless Jesus washed his feet. Jesus not only spoke of being a servant, but also demonstrated what a servant looked like, and commanded those who would follow Him to do the same.[5]

Write out Luke 22:25-27.

What does Jesus tell them?

These verses also describe something that happened during the Last Supper, after Jesus had washed the disciples' feet. Jesus reminds them again that He came to serve, and that they should do the same. There are many different ways that you can serve others on your team. Have you thought of helping to put out equipment before practice or to pick it up after practice (especially those areas you are not specifically responsible for)? Spending time with a friend in need? Giving someone a ride even if it is out of your way? Not making underclassmen feel so insignificant, but making them feel like they are an important part of the team?

Write down some ways that you can serve others around you.

Day 5
Tell the World–Being His Witness
Have you ever been on a team that you were really proud of? Or do you have a high school, college, or professional team that is "your" team? You want to watch every game. You cheer for the team. Play your heart out for the team. And at the end of the season if the team wins the championship, you want everyone

to know, and you join in the celebration of winning. Even if you have not personally experienced this on your team or a team you follow, it is a hope and goal of every athlete to "win it all" one day. And on that day you want the whole world to know! As a Christian, you possess the greatest news ever given to mankind, more important and more powerful than any news of a team winning the championship. You have the opportunity and privilege to tell the whole world about the One who loves you and died for you so that you could be in a right relationship with the Father.

Write out Luke 19:10.

One of the things Jesus came to do was to seek and save the lost. Who are the lost? The people who do not know Jesus. He had a heart of compassion for people and saw that they needed love, acceptance, forgiveness, and healing. Jesus continues to seek and save the lost through us (those who believe in Him). According to the following verses, what are we commanded to do?

    Mark 16:15

    Matthew 28:18-20

To do all that we are commanded would be an impossible challenge if we had to do this on our own, in our own strength and power. How can we go and tell others about Jesus? God does not leave us to do the job by ourselves. He gives us the power and the desire to obey Him.

Write out Acts 1:8.

When do you receive power, and who gives the power?

After you receive God's power, what happens?

It is the greatest calling to share God's love and forgiveness with others. But remember that Jesus never calls you to do something and then leaves you to do it alone. He lives inside each believer, and He is the One who lives His life through you.

Amy often felt a little scared when she shared about the Lord. She was afraid of rejection and being labeled a fanatic or weirdo. In all the times she shared about the Lord, she really doesn't remember anyone making fun of her, but still, that fear was usually right there when she shared. Once while she was traveling by bus across the country, she sat next to a lady who was from Peru. It just so happened that Amy was returning home after spending several weeks in Peru! As the two women shared about their lives and talked about Peru, the opportunity came up for Amy to share her faith with the other woman. Amy never forgot the woman's desire and longing to understand and believe what Amy was telling her. As far as Amy knows, the woman did not give her life to the Lord that day, but she did hear about the Lord's love and forgiveness.

List some of the things that hinder you from sharing your faith.

How can you overcome these?

Think of those people you know who do not know Christ. They are missing out on the most incredible relationship they could have. Write out what the following verses say the benefits are to becoming a Christian:

John 1:12 and 1 John 3:1

Psalm 103:3

Romans 5:1

Romans 8:38, 39

Ephesians 3:17-19

1 John 5:13

Galatians 5:22, 23

Besides these benefits, someone who becomes a Christian is given direction, meaning, and purpose for her life, and is able to experience God's power to change her life.

How many people does God want to come to know Him? (Read 2 Peter 3:9)

God does not want anyone to die without knowing Him. He wants everyone to come to Him, and He has called you to tell others about Him. So how do you do this?

Have you ever been around people who like to brag about how good they are and how no one can beat them or their team? What do you think when you hear "trash talk"? Do you talk trash to try and gain a mental edge over your opponent? It is one thing to say you can do something, but it is different to show someone you can do it.

Actions speak louder than words. What you say is important, but how you live tells more about what you believe than what you say. In any sport, it is not enough to say or think that you are the best player or best team, you must show it. And in your life, it is not so much what you say, but how you live that will show others what you believe. The best combination in sports and life is to have your words match your life. (But even if you are a good player or your team is good, it does not give you the right to put others down. There is maturity in showing humility.)

Jesus lived out His beliefs. Rebecca Pippert, in her book *Out of the Salt Shaker and Into the World*, wrote, "Why did Jesus so stress and demonstrate the necessity of a life that bears the stamp of profound love? Jesus said it reveals His Father's essence. Jesus was not loving and kind to others merely because He happened to be warm and considerate and had good role models at home. He loved people the way He did because He was doing His

Relationships as a Christian

Father's will and demonstrating His character."[6]

Jesus spoke words of love, and He demonstrated a life of love. Verbal and non-verbal communication are both very important. As Jesus lives His life through you, remember that whomever you touch, Jesus touches. You do not simply give the gospel, you **are** the gospel.

As you develop relationships with friends, teammates, coaches, opponents, and fans, you will have opportunities to share Christ. List some natural ways you can share Christ with others.

Summary of the Week
This chapter has looked at how we relate as a Christian. Our lives should reflect who we really are on the inside. God is at work in our lives, making us more and more like His Son by teaching us how to correctly relate with each other through forgiving, loving, and serving each other. As we reflect the character of Jesus, we are giving a right estimate of who God really is to those around us. We are glorifying God through our lives. May you cooperate with the Lord as He changes your heart to reflect His heart, and as He uses you to impact your family, friends, teammates, coaches, and others.

5
Relationships as a Female

As we have seen throughout these chapters, God created us to be in relationships. We have the need for a relationship with God (vertical) and with others (horizontal). Relationships are not optional; they are required for our growth and development as human beings. Most of the time relationships encourage and support us while helping us to learn more about ourselves. However, there may be times when you are tempted to substitute your relationship with another person for your need to have a relationship with God. It won't work. Only God can satisfy the need for a relationship with Him! It is not a sin to want relationships; that is how you were created. However, when we put another person in the place of our relationship with God, we are worshiping that person.

This chapter is going to look at several areas of relationships: the different levels of friendship; healthy vs. unhealthy relationships; dating; and maintaining healthy relationships.

Day 1

Levels of Friendship

How many friends do you have in your life? Are they all your "best friend," or are you closer to some friends than you are to others? Most people will agree that there are different types of friendships. In their book *Friends and Friendship*, Jerry and Mary White explore several categories of friendship.[1] Following is a description of those categories.

Some people you may recognize from a class or may have seen around campus, but you may not know them well. You may not even know their last name. These people are **acquaintances**. They aren't really friends. You make acquaintances every day, and it is the largest category of relationships you'll have.

Others you may see regularly at work, in a study group, or in the weight room, but you have minimal outside social contact with them. You know them by first name but don't know much else about them. These are **casual friends**, and you probably have a lot of them in your life. Your relationship is probably focused around a specific activity. The contact you have may be more superficial. Casual friends usually don't meet the deeper needs we have for relationships.

Close friendships can include people at school or work that you see on a regular basis, neighbors, teammates, or people involved in your Bible study group. These relationships usually develop out of mutual involvement in an activity or a common goal. There is generally a lot of social contact, and discussions may be of a more personal nature. If the activity is finished or the goal is met, the friendship may change to that of a casual friend, an acquaintance, or the friendship may continue and grow.

One type of close friendship is the *personal friendship*. These types of friendships are kept going outside of work, school, or other activities. You are able to discuss problems with the person, feel comfortable sharing feelings, and spend more time developing this type of relationship than the others previously mentioned. This relationship will continue for years even if the two of you move apart. You both want to continue contact and choose to stay in touch.

Another type of close friendship is the *associate friendship*. Usually, associates are co-workers, people from church, relatives, or others that we have something in common with, such as belonging to an organization, group, or family.

A *mentor friendship* is the third type of close friendship. A mentor is one who disciples you, helps guide you during a period of time in your life, and contributes to you as a person. A mentor relationship often occurs for a specific amount of time with a particular goal for the mentoring.

Finally, the last level of friendship is that of an **intimate friend**. An intimate friend, or best friend, is someone you share deep feelings, thoughts, hopes, and dreams with. You are energized around this type of friend and maintain the relationship over a long period of time. Intimate friendship is developed slowly over time and is a long-term investment. Most people can only maintain a small number of intimate friendships because of the time and energy they require.

Now take some time to evaluate your friendships. In each category, write down the names of people in your life who best fit that description.

Acquaintances:

_____   _____

_____   _____

_____   _____

Casual friends:

_____   _____

_____   _____

_____   _____

Close friends

Associate friendships:

_____   _____

_____   _____

_____   _____

Personal friendships:

_____   _____

_____   _____

Mentor friendships:

_____   _____

Intimate friends:

_____   _____

_____   _____

Hopefully you were able to write down the name of at least one person in each category. If so, then you have some balance in your relationships. If not, then you may want to consider how you might develop relationships in some of the categories so that you do not have most of your relationships at one or two particular levels of friendship. Now let's take a look at some of the reasons why it is important to have friends. Read the following verses and write out what the benefit is to having friends.

Ecclesiastes 4:9-12

Proverbs 27:6

Galatians 6:2

Remember that Jesus was a person like you, and He also had the need for relationships. We are going to take a look at who met the different levels of relationship in the life of Jesus. Read the following verses and write in the space provided the name(s) of those who were involved in the life of Jesus.

Acquaintances
(Matthew 14:13-21; John 9:1-7; John 4:4-26)

Casual friends
(Matthew 8:14-15; Luke 19:1-10; John 3:1-21)

Close friends
(Matthew 27:57-61; Mark 3:13-19; John 3:13-17; 11:1-5)

Intimate friends
(Matthew 11:27; 17:1-2)

It is important to keep in mind that Jesus knew the hearts of all people. While He was on earth, Jesus spent varying amounts of time with different people. But Jesus loves all people the same. He cares deeply about every one of His followers.

What type of relationship do you have with Jesus? Maybe Jesus is more like an acquaintance to you. You've heard a lot about Him from other people, maybe you've even read about Him in the Bible, but you do not have the kind of "best friend" relationship that we are talking about. Check next to the type of friendship that best describes the relationship you have right now with Jesus Christ:

_____ Acquaintance
_____ Casual friendship
_____ Close friendship
_____ Intimate friendship

If you do not currently have an intimate friendship with Jesus, write down what would help the relationship move to the next level. For example, spending more time in prayer or learning more about who Jesus is by reading the Bible. Remember, Jesus **wants** an intimate relationship with you!

Day 2
Having people at the different levels of friendship will help you to maintain balance in your relationships. There is not one person who can meet all of your needs for friendship. However, there may be times when you start to depend too much on one person for your friendship needs. When this happens, problems can result. This section will look at some examples of unhealthy relationships, how unhealthy relationships develop, and what to do if you recognize signs of an unhealthy relationship in the life of yourself or someone else.

Unhealthy Relationships
Jeanette was not the life of the party, but she was well-liked by her high school classmates. She was always helpful to others, and appeared to always be in a positive mood. If you were having a bad day, Jeanette was the one person who could encourage you. She did well in school and was consistently named to the honor roll. During her junior year, Jeanette was asked out by Alan, who was a senior and captain of the football team.

Although she had several friends and dated occasionally, once Alan asked her out, Jeanette was part of the popular crowd. Alan took Jeanette to parties, and she even got to know the popular kids from other schools. He showered her with attention and always sent her notes, cards, and sometimes flowers to let her know how much she meant to him. Jeanette was on top of the world.

After dating for a few months, Jeanette began to see a side of Alan she did not know existed. It was generally known that Alan had a temper, but it had only been a problem on the football field. Alan had even been ejected from a game once for punching another player. After a football game in which he did not play well, Alan was in a nasty mood. Jeanette and Alan were riding together to a post-game party when Alan began to go on and on about his poor performance. Jeanette tried to encourage him by telling him it would be OK, that he would play better next time.

Alan screamed, "What do you know about it? I don't want you to say another word!"

Jeanette tried to explain that she was only trying to help. As soon as she began speaking, Alan reached back his hand and slapped Jeanette across the face. Tears streaming down her face, Jeanette sat in stunned silence as Alan fumed. Once they arrived at the party, Alan apologized profusely. "I just lost control. I'll never do that again, I promise. You know how much you mean to me."

Jeanette believed Alan. After all, he had been so kind and attentive, and she thought that he really did care about her. Things were fine for a few weeks, but eventually Alan "lost control" again. This time he shoved Jeanette against the car after she tried to take the keys from him because he had been drinking. Again, Alan apologized and promised he wouldn't do it again. Soon, Jeanette's friends noticed that she was more withdrawn and did not smile as much. Although she was still dating Alan, she did not talk about him as often as she did when they had started dating. One of her friends noticed some bruises on Jeanette's arms while they were changing for gym class. Jeanette explained that she and Alan sometimes wrestled and he "forgets how strong he is."

This is an example of an abusive relationship. Often, a person in an abusive relationship believes that she may have done something wrong to deserve the abuse, or she may believe that if she stays with the person, she can help them to change. Abuse is not always physical. Abuse can also be verbal and emotional. If you need to, review Day 3 of the section on "Identity as a Female" (Chapter 2) and effects of abuse. If you are in an abusive relationship, you may be afraid of leaving the relationship, either out of fear of what the other person might do or fear of being alone.

Unhealthy relationships are not always abusive. Sometimes relationships can start off as healthy, normal friendships, but develop into a relationship that is unhealthy in a different way. Here is an example.

Jill had always been a quiet girl. She was an honor roll student, excelled in sports and was a "good kid." She had become a Christian at the age of 7 and attended church on a regular basis. It was no surprise to anyone when Jill received an athletic scholarship to attend college. She was so good at several sports, she had a number of scholarship offers to choose from! What most people didn't know about Jill was that inside she was actually insecure. For years she tried to gain acceptance and approval from her parents, friends, and coaches by succeeding in sports and in the classroom. When she arrived at college, Jill found out that all of her teammates were just as good an athlete as she was. In fact, some were even better! Suddenly, the talents that Jill had relied on did not win her the same praise and sense of identity that they did in junior high and high school. Her insecurity grew until Jill found herself feeling lonely, unsure and longing for acceptance.

That's when Jill began to spend more time with one of her teammates, Becky. Becky was a team captain, outgoing, popular, and two years older than Jill. Becky encouraged Jill during practices, helped her to feel part of the team, and introduced Jill to other friends. Within a few months Becky and Jill were spending most of their time together. When they weren't at practice, they would go to the student lounge or library and study together. At night they would watch TV, go to a movie, or spend hours talking. Some nights Jill and Becky would be talking so late together that Jill would just spend the night at Becky's apartment rather than walk back to her dorm.

Soon Jill and Becky began to spend all of their time together, and Jill even turned down invitations to study or go out with other people because she didn't want Becky to feel left out or get upset. Jill began to feel frustrated when she couldn't spend time with Becky. Other people began to feel uncomfortable when they were around Jill and Becky, because the two of them would laugh at "inside jokes" that others didn't understand, or would show physical affection to each other that seemed inappropriate, like hugging each other for long periods of time. It wasn't long before rumors started on the team that Jill and Becky were in a lesbian relationship.

What happened in Jill and Becky's relationship is not that uncommon. What started out as a positive friendship turned into an emotionally dependent relationship. Sometimes an emotionally dependent relationship crosses physical boundaries and leads into a homosexual relationship. Although Jill was a Christian, she was lonely and insecure when she moved away to college. Rather than relying on her relationship with Christ, Jill looked to Becky for stability and acceptance. The relationship with Becky prevented Jill from developing other relationships and growing spiritually. Often a person in an emotionally dependent relationship adjusts major areas of her life in an effort to please the other person. Emotional dependency can happen in same-sex or opposite-sex relationships. It is important to understand what emotional dependency is, how to recognize it, and what to do if you or someone you know is in an emotionally dependent relationship.

What is an Unhealthy Relationship?
Any relationship where we put a person as central to our existence over God is unhealthy. It is also a sin, whether or not there is any sexual contact. When the relationship begins to be the most important thing in your life, you place a priority on the relationship and begin to make all of your decisions with that relationship in mind. The presence of the other person is necessary to your personal stability or security. You want (or try to get) all of your needs met through one person. Everything else is secondary, even God. The relationship has become an idol in

your life. You are worshiping the **creation** rather than the **creator**. If something (or someone) does not draw you closer to God, it (or they) will draw you away from God.

In her book *Out of Egypt*, Jeanette Howard says that an emotionally dependent relationship "usually involves two people who are completely enmeshed in each other's lives. . . .When two people are involved in dependent behavior, neither party can distinguish their own personal boundaries and life from the personhood of the other. In emotional dependency, the core of the relationship is the relationship itself."[2] Howard identifies the following as factors that can lead to emotional dependency:

> *Real or perceived rejection from significant others
> *Unfilled need for love and approval from members of the same sex
> *Rejection of feminine role and gender
> *Low self-esteem
> *Failure or unwillingness to accept maturity/adulthood, a retreat to an earlier, more secure stage of life
> *Need to be in control (this is sometimes easier to achieve in same-sex relationships)
> *Mistrust (it is easier to set up the world the way we want it than to accept what God has planned for us)
> *Loneliness (which tends to breed insecurity)
> *Anger or bitterness towards the opposite sex
> *Frustration or disillusionment with opposite-sex relationships
> *Rebellion (refusing to surrender areas of our life to God)

Howard further states that you do not need all of these characteristics to develop an emotionally dependent relationship, but if you struggle in any of these areas, you may be susceptible to emotional dependency.

TIME OUT!
Do you recognize any of these characteristics in your own life? If so, which one(s)?

Just as there are factors that can make a person susceptible to an emotionally dependent relationship, there are also signs that can help you to identify if a relationship is emotionally dependent.

Signs of Emotional Dependency:
- *Sharing "deep feelings" with someone you hardly know, achieving a superficial sense of intimacy
- *Viewing others as a threat to the relationship, and often feeling jealousy, possessiveness, and desiring exclusivity with the person
- *Preferring to spend time alone with the person and feeling frustrated when it doesn't happen
- *Becoming irrationally angry or depressed when the other person withdraws from the relationship or spends time with others
- *Losing interest in other relationships
- *Spending a great deal of effort, money, and resources to spend time with the person
- *Cannot go through the day without talking with the person (calling frequently, visiting)
- *Experiencing romantic or sexual feelings about the person, leading to fantasies about the person

*Becoming preoccupied with the other person's appearance, personality, problems, and interests
*Unwilling to make short- or long-range plans that do not include the other person
*Unable to see the other person's faults realistically ("she's wonderful"/"he'd never do that")
*Displaying physical affection beyond what is appropriate for a friendship
*Others feeling uncomfortable, unwelcome, or embarrassed when around you and the other person
*Physical, verbal, and/or emotional abuse being hidden, excused, or minimized
*Becoming extremely defensive when others raise questions/concerns about your relationship with the other person

TIME OUT!
Do you recognize any of the symptoms of emotional dependency in any of your relationships? If so, which one(s)?

Putting It into Practice
If you find yourself in an emotionally dependent relationship, it is important to understand that there is not one person who "caused" it. There are qualities or characteristics in each of you that contributed to the emotional dependency. Following are some suggestions to start dealing with the situation.

The first step in breaking the pattern of emotional dependency is to **be honest**. Even though we all sin, the shame we sometimes feel can prevent us from being honest with God, ourselves, and others in regard to the sin in our lives. Being honest about the relationship will start you on the road to healing. Honesty with others is also important so that they can support and encourage you as you develop healthy relationships.

Confess your sin to God and ask for His forgiveness. Again, emotional dependency is a sin. You have placed a person in God's place, and you need to confess. When you do, God forgives you and restores your relationship with Him. Ask God to reclaim His place as the one you are dependent on for everything. It may also be necessary to ask forgiveness of others, especially the one you were in the relationship with. Let that person know why you are asking for their forgiveness. If he/she is not a Christian, you may have the opportunity to witness to them!

Look for **accountability**. It is important to have spiritually mature people in your life who can ask you difficult questions about your relationships to help make sure you don't fall into the same pattern again. An accountability partner can also express concerns to you about relationships or other areas of your life that you might not be aware of. This person needs to be someone you can trust and be honest with. It is also best that the person has good boundaries and understands what healthy relationships are. This will help to prevent you from becoming emotionally dependent on them. It may be important to receive additional counseling to understand what the deeper issues are in your life that have led you into emotional dependency.

The process of changing your relationships includes learning to develop **intimacy** and **boundaries** in your relationships. This means first developing intimacy in your relationship with God.

Spend time getting to know Him. Read His word and learn what He is like. You will find that as you develop intimacy with God, it will be easier to develop intimacy with other people. During the process you may need to break off any emotionally dependent relationships you are in, at least for awhile. It may also be necessary to seek counseling to help you in the process.

Day 3
The previous section mentioned that it is possible for an emotionally dependent relationship to develop into a homosexual relationship. Unfortunately, there are many stereotypes that claim female athletes are lesbians, or participating in athletics or certain sports will lead you into homosexuality. Competing in sports does not "make" someone gay. However, it would also be wrong to say that all female athletes are only involved in heterosexual relationships. It is important to understand this issue, which is quickly becoming one of the most prominent issues in society today, and how it might affect you as an athlete.

Crossing the Line
There is an abundance of gay characters portrayed in television and movies, as well as books and propaganda aimed at convincing the public that people are born gay. There are churches today that "bless" homosexual unions and encourage a homosexual relationship between two people that is loving, monogamous, and committed. In fact, individuals who do not agree with homosexuality are often labeled as homophobic and told that if they cannot accept this "alternative lifestyle," then *they* are the ones who need help.

Relationships as a Female

The contrasting, anti-homosexual viewpoint among some people who call themselves Christians is just as damaging. They carry signs with slogans such as "God hates fags" and "AIDS is God's solution for homosexuality" at various pro-gay rallies and conferences. These people claim that homosexuals are perverts and condemned to hell. How do we determine what to believe about homosexuality? Where can we turn for honest answers?

When it comes to homosexuality, the issue is not as ambiguous as one might think. Scripture has always been clear on the issue of homosexuality. Read the following verses and write down what each says about this issue.

* Leviticus 18:22

* Leviticus 20:13 (It is important to keep in mind that this was the same punishment to be used for those who committed adultery or cursed a parent.)

* Romans 1:24-27

* 1 Corinthians 6:9-11

There are also references to homosexuality in Genesis 19:1-20, Judges 19:1-25, and 1 Timothy 1:9-11. The Bible never portrays homosexual relationships in a positive way and it condemns **any** sexual act outside the marriage relationship. This does not mean that if two people of the same sex are "married" in a church then their relationship is approved by God. Biblical marriage is defined as marriage between one man and one woman. The next section will examine the issue of sexual purity more closely.

Although some research studies have suggested that homosexuality is genetic in nature, there is no clear scientific evidence to support this theory. The research that has been done is questionable at best. [3,4]

Factors that Influence

What "causes" someone to be gay? There is no easy answer to this question, although there is not one single factor that causes homosexuality. Some people believe that homosexuals are born with the orientation to same-sex relationships, although research does not support these conclusions. Most Christians who help people out of the homosexual lifestyle agree on certain common factors that seem to influence the lives of women involved in homosexuality. Even then, many people experience these factors and are never involved in a homosexual relationship. Keep in mind that the following are factors that can *influence* whether someone is susceptible and drawn to same-sex relationships, but do not guarantee that will happen.

* A relationship between a mother and daughter that is not nurturing and protective. The mother may be critical and domineering, self-absorbed and manipulative, or weak and ineffective. Rather than develop her identity as a woman based on the influence of her mother, the girl looks for affirmation and nurturing in other female relationships. This can lead to emotional dependency, as mentioned in the previous section, or a lesbian relationship.[2]

Relationships as a Female 141

* A relationship between a father and daughter that does not affirm the daughter's femininity and gender is also a factor. Maybe the father wanted a son, and made several remarks to this effect. Or he was emotionally distant or absent altogether from the family and did not teach his daughter how to relate to the opposite sex. Or he may have been abusive. In these situations the girl learns that men do not provide the security and nurturing that she needs. Without a healthy male role model early on, females do not learn how to relate effectively to men. Their response may be turning to other women to get these needs met.[2, 4]

* Peer influence can also be a factor. If a girl enjoys activities that are not considered "feminine," peers can sometimes tease or make hurtful comments that are remembered. She may internalize these comments and feel rejected because of her gender, or feel that she should have been a boy instead of a girl. Traumatic events, such as sexual abuse and emotional and verbal abuse, can lead to a sense of shame and destroy the ability to trust others. If the abuse was perpetrated by a male, it can lead to a fear of and distancing from men in order to protect oneself. Not all women who are abused end up in a homosexual relationship, but there are some estimates that as many as 80% of lesbians have been sexually abused in some way. Certainly an incident as traumatic as sexual abuse impacts a person's sexuality in a very profound way.[2, 3, 4]

These are just a few of the factors that can influence whether a person becomes involved in a homosexual relationship. Although the Bible does not say anything about sexual orientation, it does address the issue of sexual behavior. Having an attraction to other women does not mean that you are a lesbian, but there are likely to be some underlying psychological issues that contributed to that attraction. It is true that keeping such feelings inside will not make them "disappear," and may in fact affect your ability to develop relationships. Going to a Christian counselor may help you to understand some of the influences on same-sex attraction and learn how to develop boundaries in relationships.

Within the area of athletics, there is sometimes a subculture of women who are involved in homosexuality. Again, this is not to say that all female athletes are lesbians, but given some of the factors that may contribute to involvement in homosexual relationships, it makes sense that if a woman is looking for emotional fulfillment and nurturing from a female, she might find such a relationship with a teammate or coach. This does not mean that you should quit athletics or trade in your sneakers for a sewing kit. The purpose of this study is to raise awareness of some of the stereotypes as well as pressures you might experience as a female athlete.

Unfortunately, there is not enough space in this section to cover all of the issues related to this topic. For more in-depth study on this subject, several resources are listed at the end of the book.

Day 4
The Dating Game
What do you think of when you hear the word "dating"?

Relationships as a Female

The Bible really doesn't deal specifically with dating, because in those times marriages were arranged by the parents. Can you imagine your mom or dad picking out the guy you were going to marry? The purpose of dating has changed somewhat over the years. Dating today is sometimes more of a social activity rather than a time to prepare for marriage.

Name some reasons why people your age date.

Maybe you are someone who enjoys dating. You have fun getting to know different people and enjoy going out and doing things. Or maybe the thought of dating scares you, because you haven't dated much and feel unsure and embarrassed around guys. You may not be interested in dating right now but feel pressured to date because your friends do. You may be worried that if you aren't dating someone you will spend more time at home alone on weekends. It is important to have the right motives to date someone. If you are only dating someone because you feel pressured to, then you are probably not ready to date.

In the section "Identity as a Female," you learned that you are created as a sexual being, with the capacity for thoughts and feelings that are related to your sexuality. Remember, as sexual beings we are created to enjoy the act of sex within the marriage relationship. Though there is much political debate today as to what the definition of marriage should be, Scripture is very clear. God's plan for sexual relationships is found in Genesis 2:24: *"For this reason a man will leave his father and mother and be united to his wife, and they will become one flesh.*" God's intention is for a sexual relationship to occur in marriage between one man and one woman. Any sexual relationship outside of marriage is sexual immorality. Sexual immorality includes any sexual act committed outside of marriage, with either someone of the same or opposite sex. In other words, it is sin.

Sexual immorality cannot separate you from God's love or keep you beyond His reach. Romans 8:38 states that "...*neither death nor life, neither angels nor demons, neither the present nor the future, nor any powers, neither height nor depth, nor anything else in all creation, will be able to separate us from the love of God that is in Christ Jesus our Lord.*"

Read the following verses and write out what they say about sexual immorality:
 Hebrews 13:4

 1 Corinthians 6:13b

 1 Corinthians 6:18, 19

 1 Corinthians 10:12, 13

 1 Thessalonians 4:3, 4

Although sexual immorality is a sin, it is not an unpardonable sin. God is impartial when it comes to sin. He does not think that one sin is worse than another (1 Timothy 1:9, 10). In 1 Corinthians 6:9-11, we read that sexual immorality is forgiven like any other sin: "*...that is what some of you were. But you were washed, you were sanctified, you were justified in the name of the Lord Jesus Christ and by the Spirit of our God.*" Sexual immorality is no better and no worse than any other sin, but it is still sin.

If you have committed sexual immorality at any time in your life, it is important to remember that God will forgive you. First John 1:9 states, "*If we confess our sins, He is faithful and just and will forgive us our sins and cleanse us from all unrighteousness.*"

"What's the Big Deal?"
Some people don't agree that a person should wait to have sex until they are married. They come up with many reasons why it is OK not to wait to have sex until marriage. For example:
> "We really love each other, and that's what counts."
> "We're being safe, and besides, we think we'll get married someday."
> "Everyone is having sex, and I don't want to be the only virgin left in the world."
> "If God made sex, then He must want us to experience it."
> "What if I never get married? Then you're saying I can't have sex at all, and that's not fair!"

Some of these arguments may sound pretty good. In fact, you may have used one or more of these statements to defend your decision to have premarital sex. The problem is, each of these statements is based on messages that come from the world, not from God. It is true, sex was created by God to be enjoyed by a man and woman, but only within the marriage relationship. You may think that your boyfriend is "the one," but be careful. Don't deceive yourself into lowering God's standard because of a "feeling." If your boyfriend or fiancé really is your future husband, use the time while you are dating and during the engagement relationship to get to know each other better, learn about the relationship, and enjoy each other. Having sex before marriage is taking the relationship to a level it wasn't intended to go to.

There can be peer pressure about having sex as well. It can be frustrating to feel that you are "missing out" on something that everyone else is enjoying. Consider the number of television shows and movies that portray teenage or young adult relationships. The majority depict the characters having a sexual relationship, but rarely do they ever show the consequences of that relationship. How many movies have you seen in which a couple has sex and then one of the partners contracts a venereal disease? Or the girl gets pregnant unexpectedly and aborts the baby, only to have guilt and depression later in life? Remember that God allows us the freedom to make choices, but He also promises that when we disobey His Word, there will be consequences (Deuteronomy 11:26-28). Maybe not tomorrow or next week, but at some time in your life.

Read John 8:1-11. It is the story of a woman who is caught in adultery. Although the religious men wanted to stone her (literally throwing stones at her body to kill her) as punishment, which was required by Jewish law, Jesus had a different response. He said to the religious men, *"If any one of you is without sin, let him be the first to throw a stone at her"* (v. 7). None of them could, because they all knew that at one time or another, they had sinned too! Although Jesus did not agree with what the woman had done, He made it clear that sexual sins are no better or worse than any other sin, but it is still sin! After her accusers left, Jesus told the woman, *"Neither do I condemn you...go now and leave your life of sin"* (v. 11). In other words, change your ways!

TIME OUT!
Are there sexual sins from the past that you have been thinking about during this chapter? If so, the Holy Spirit may be convicting you. If you have not asked God to forgive you before, take some time now to pray. Confess the sin(s) to God, ask His forgiveness, and choose to lead your life committed to His ways.

Keeping God's Standard-Maintaining Sexual Purity
Do you know the best way to boil a frog? If you place a frog in a pot of boiling water, it will jump right out because it can tell right away that the hot water is a danger. However, if you place the frog in a pot of lukewarm water on the stove and slowly heat it, the frog will stay put and will eventually boil to death. Why? Because frogs adjust to temperature changes in their surroundings, and if the change is subtle enough the frog will adapt to the change without realizing how dangerous the situation has become.

Although we are much different from frogs, the same principle applies when it comes to sexual temptations. You may have been raised with strong morals and taught appropriate boundaries in dating relationships, but it can be difficult to maintain sexual purity when you are actually dating someone. It can be easy to gradually adjust your standard for what is "OK contact" so that after a while, you (just like the frog) don't realize that you are in a dangerous situation.

Take some time to answer the following question. What type of contact do you consider appropriate when you are dating someone? (Holding hands, kissing, french kissing, etc.)

How about if you were engaged to marry the person? Would the limits change? If so, why?

Now consider this. If you knew that a friend was dating the guy whom you were going to marry someday, how far would you want her to go with him? Would it be OK with you if they were making out all the time? Probably not. Since you may not know for sure right now who you are going to get married to, remember that if you get married someday, your dating relationships are really preparing you for your marriage.

Tips
To help maintain your standards of physical contact on a date, first know what situations or activities are going to tempt you to go beyond the limits you have set for yourself and the relationship. For example, if you tend to spend a lot of time kissing when you are alone together, and kissing eventually leads to fondling each other, it is best to avoid situations when you are completely alone. Go out with other couples, spend time as a couple in public places, or only allow him to come to your house when someone else is there (the thought of Mom or Dad walking into the room during a make-out session has helped many young couples maintain boundaries!).

Talk over your thoughts and convictions on dating with your

boyfriend. He needs to know where you are coming from and the two of you need to decide what the limits are going to be. Remember that you are each responsible for your own actions, even in "the heat of the moment."

Avoid activities or situations that will expose you to images or thoughts that you will dwell on. Certain R-rated movies, sexually graphic music, and pornographic material (magazines or certain Internet sites) all have the ability to get you aroused and focused on sexual thoughts and fantasies.

Encourage activities which will help draw both of you closer to God. Spend time attending church, youth group, or a fellowship group together. Help others by volunteering time at a nursing home or homeless shelter. Have group dates with several other couples doing something fun. These kinds of activities will not only help you to maintain boundaries with each other, but will allow you to watch how he relates to other people.

Make a dating covenant. The Southern Baptist Convention started a program called "True Love Waits." It asks young people to make the commitment not to have a sexual relationship with anyone until they are married. Thousands of young people have made the commitment so far! These young people are making a commitment to God and to their future spouse.

Day 5
Healthy Relationships
We have spent a lot of time discussing unhealthy relationships, but it is just as important to understand what a **healthy** relation-

ship looks like. Jerry and Mary White define a friend as "a trusted confidant to whom I am mutually drawn as a companion and an ally, whose love for me is not dependent on my performance, and whose influence draws me closer to God."[1] Certain qualities are usually evident in a healthy relationship:

Honesty. You are able to confront each other and ask hard questions when you see the other person doing something wrong/questionable. You can risk saying something the other person might not want to hear, and you can disagree with each other without feeling threatened or afraid of losing the relationship. You can be yourself, and do not feel a need to change who you are (what you look like, how you act, the way you do things) to please the other person.

Boundaries. You can say no without feeling guilty. You can ask the other person for help without manipulating them to get what you want. You share feelings with each other, but don't take on feelings for the other person. You both have other friends, interests, hobbies, etc. You are happy for and encourage other relationships for the other person without jealousy or fear of "losing" him/her. You don't feel that you have to compete with other people for time with your friend, and you enjoy having others around when you are together.

Established over time. There is no "quick and easy" way to build trust in a relationship. This happens over time. Trying to achieve intimacy too quickly can ruin a relationship. Enjoy your time with the other person rather than trying to rush to a deeper level.

Desire God's best for each other. You have a mutual desire to see

Relationships as a Female

the other person seek God's will for his/her life, and you rejoice with that person when good things happen to him/her. You are genuinely concerned with how your friend is doing, not preoccupied with getting your own needs met. You can also ask for help from the other person without making them or you feel guilty.

Have fun. You can laugh together, enjoy activities, and find pleasure in spending time with the other person. Spend time doing things each of you enjoy so that you step out of your "comfort zone" and try something new!

Mutual love of Jesus Christ. Your closest relationships will likely be with other Christians, because that is the most important thing in each of your lives. Their influence will help you grow in your relationship with God. There are some things that will help strengthen those relationships. Both of you are involved in fellowship, individual prayer, and Bible study, and maybe even a small group. The other person doesn't encourage you in activities or relationships that will turn you away from your relationship with Jesus. Not all relationships you have will probably be with other Christians, but your relationships with other people should draw both of you closer to Him in some way. Even with non-believers, they will at least witness your life as you live and work in a manner that shines the light of Christ to them. It is important to be able to relate to both males and females in a healthy way. Developing relationships is how you learn to communicate with others, and will allow you to identify the qualities you desire in a potential mate.

TIME OUT!
List the qualities of healthy relationships that you need to improve in your own life. Spend time thinking and praying about your relationships.

Healthy relationships begin with healthy people. Not in the physical sense necessarily, but spiritually and emotionally. Watch to see if others demonstrate the fruit of the Spirit mentioned in Galatians 5:22, 23. You will be able to tell by their actions where the person is at in his/her Christian walk. Having a healthy relationship with someone does not mean you will never have disagreements or that there won't be any problems at all. On the contrary, in a healthy relationship you have the freedom to disagree with others.

What do you think of when you hear the word "fellowship"? Is this a term that you only associate with church, choir practice, and Bible study? The word for fellowship in the Bible is the Greek word *koinonia*, which means "sharing in common." It means that we have a common bond with other Christians. That bond is the Lord Jesus Christ! When we are with other Christians we are together as members of the Body of Christ. This is a reason for celebration! There are Christians around the world who do not have the freedom to gather and fellowship with other Christians for fear of persecution, imprisonment, or worse. Take some time and thank God for the freedom you have to worship Him and to fellowship with other believers!

How to Help Others Without Hurting Yourself
Have you ever had to confront someone? It is not always a

Relationships as a Female

pleasant experience. Yet sometimes it takes the willingness of a friend to say what we don't want to hear in order to recognize sin in our lives. Take Chris, for instance. Kelly and several of her teammates noticed that Chris, another player on the team, was involved in what seemed to be an emotionally dependent relationship with another girl. Kelly and her friends were concerned because of the changes they had seen in Chris. She no longer joined group social activities, was skipping class on a regular basis to be with this friend, and had even stopped attending church.

Since Kelly and Chris were both Christians, Kelly decided to approach Chris and share her concerns. Initially, Chris was very defensive. She denied that there was anything wrong or that the relationship was inappropriate. She even accused Kelly of being jealous of her new friend! When Kelly asked Chris if she was still spending daily time with God, Chris became irritated and left. Kelly was saddened by her friend's response. She was only trying to help. Later that night, Chris called Kelly. She apologized for her behavior, and told Kelly that after their conversation she had gone home and pulled out her prayer journal. It had been weeks since she had written in it, and most of the entries before that were about her relationship with her new friend. Chris thanked Kelly for taking the risk of telling her something she really didn't want to hear. Kelly agreed to check in with Chris periodically to see how she was doing with the relationship, and Chris decided to talk with one of the pastors at church about the relationship.

TIME OUT!
Think of a time when you decided to confront a friend about something. How did your friend respond?

What happened to your friendship after you confronted the person?

Read 2 John (it is the shortest book in the Bible) and notice the emphasis on truth and love in the life of a Christian. Truth and love are inseparable for the Christian. Sometimes we can focus more on truth instead of love, and vice versa. They are meant to complement each other, and both are necessary when confronting another person. When you tell people something they don't want to hear, they may choose not to agree with you, or may even avoid you so that you do not bring up the subject again. Your responsibility to them is to speak truth, but remember to do it in love. If you speak the truth but do it harshly and unlovingly, you may wound the other person and not be heard.

"Reckless words pierce like a sword, but the tongue of the wise brings healing" (Proverbs 12:18).

Here are some things to keep in mind if you are in a situation of confrontation.

Your responsibility as a Christian is to demonstrate the love of God to others in all that you do. It is not to judge others (Matthew 7:1-2), call them names, or speak negatively about them (1 Timothy 4:12). Jesus went out of His way to associate with "sinners" in His day, especially those who were thought of as social outcasts or undesirable by the community (Matthew 11:19). Jesus also had strong words for the "religious" leaders of His day who judged the behavior of others and had an attitude of arrogance (Matthew 15:7-9). Jesus responded in a manner that drew others to Him while always upholding His standards.

Relationships as a Female

As His followers, we are to respond to others in a manner that will draw them to Jesus.

Make sure that you are practicing what you preach. Before you approach anyone else about their unhealthy relationships, evaluate your own life and make sure that your own relationships are healthy, balanced, supportive, and honoring Christ (Matthew 7:3-5). Are you growing in your relationship with Christ? Do you have someone that you are accountable to?

Be willing to share about your own struggles, even if it is not the same struggle your friend is having. If you are vulnerable with them, your honesty and openness may earn their trust and encourage them to open up to you about their struggles. Keep in mind that all of us have areas of struggle in our lives (Romans 7:23). It is a blessing to be able to use the difficult times in your own life to help others.

Accept the person where they are; don't reject them because of sin in their life. When it comes to helping others, make sure that you are going to them in an attitude of love, not to judge or condemn them. Be careful about making assumptions based on what you *think* you know about the relationship or what you have heard from others. It is best to talk to the individual and express your concerns or to find out what is going on. If you know someone who is in a sinful relationship, it is important to remember that you are no better or worse than that person. By taking a balanced and compassionate approach you will let the person see that you are concerned for them and are available to help. Quoting Scripture alone probably won't help the person to deal with the feelings they have, and they may become defensive or deny that anything is going on.

If you believe that a fellow Christian is engaged in sinful behavior, follow the guidelines set forth in Matthew 18:15. Go to the person in private and confront him or her about the behavior. Do this gently, in a way that expresses your concern for them.

Pray for the person and your friendship with them. You will not be able to "change" them by anything you say or do. It is only the Holy Spirit that convicts and changes people's hearts, not you.

6
Relationships as an Athlete

As an athlete, you have many relationships that are somehow related to your sport. Your relationships to teammates, coaches, officials, fans, and opponents are all different. Of course, the relationships that are most influential are typically those with whom you spend the most time. This section will focus on two of the most important relationships for an athlete: teammates and coaches.

Day 1
Part of the Team
What is a team? *Webster's Dictionary* defines a team as "a group of people working together in a coordinated effort; to join in a cooperative effort." The relationships of the players on a team can help or hinder progress towards a goal. In the Bible there are many examples of people successfully working together toward a goal, and these groups have three noticeable traits:

1. They are used to accomplish God's work.
2. They demonstrate God's power and love to others.
3. They both receive and give blessings.

Read Genesis 1.

There are three main characters: Adam, Eve, and God. This threesome might be considered the first "team." Adam and Eve's goal was to take care of the creation God had made. Adam and Eve even had the first "team conflict" when they hid from God and then argued about who was responsible for eating the forbidden fruit! With the story of Adam and Eve we are shown that God places a priority on relationships, both with Himself and with other people.

Read Genesis 6:9-22.

Noah and his family were the first "amphibious" team. Their goal was to build an ark to escape the flood, take on board a male and female of every kind of animal, and provide a faithful remnant of God's people so that God's purposes would be accomplished. Imagine spending 40 days and nights in a small boat with seven of your teammates and a zoo full of animals!

Perhaps one of the most vivid examples of teamwork recorded in the Bible is found in Exodus 17:8-13. The scene is a crucial battle between Israel and one of its enemies, the Amalekites. Read Exodus 17:8-13 and then answer the following questions:

Who do you think is the most important character in this story?

Why?

Joshua and the Israelites were only able to defeat the Amalekites if Moses held up his hands. Since Moses could not do it by himself, he needed Aaron and Hur to help him. This is a prime example of teamwork. The battle would not have been won if any one of those men was not doing his job. Each one was very important if the Israelites were going to win!

Which character do you most identify with?

Why?

Think of a time during a recent practice or game when you felt tired or frustrated, unable to keep going. You may have even questioned why you spend your time at practice since the coach doesn't play you, or you may have thought about quitting. What or who kept you going? Was there a teammate or a coach who was like Aaron or Hur to you, someone who encouraged you to stay with it?

All of us are expected to care for each other and encourage each other whenever possible, especially in regard to our faith (1 Thessalonians 5:11). This is one way that as Christians we can fill our role in the body of Christ and accomplish the three traits mentioned earlier: accomplish God's purposes, demonstrate God's love to others, and give and receive blessings.

Write down the name of at least one person on your team you will encourage this week:

Just as we discussed in Chapter 1 that God chose you to be on His team, your coach chose you to be on his or her team! The coach believes that you have something to contribute to the team, something that will help make the team better! It may be your athletic talent, your encouragement of others, your ability to be a team player, or the positive influence you have on others! In the next section we will study the importance of the role you play on your team, and how you can improve.

TIME OUT!
Who on your team is like Joshua, always in the game and leading the team in battle?

Who on the team do you consider to be like Aaron or Hur, who encourage and support others but don't always get into the game?

Even though some people on the team are more noticeable than others, keep in mind that each has a very important role. Without Aaron, Hur, or Moses, the Israelites might not have won the battle. And God was the one giving the directions!

"Do nothing out of selfish ambition or vain conceit, but in humility consider others better than yourselves. Each of you should look not only to your own interests, but also to the interests of others" (Philippians 2:3, 4).

Look for ways that you can encourage others on the team. It may mean spending extra time after practice helping a teammate with free throws or a jump shot, or going for an extra run with

Relationships as an Athlete

a teammate to help her get in shape. Other practical ideas include giving verbal support and encouragement, writing an encouraging note to the person that includes a Scripture, or praying for the person on a regular basis.

"Therefore encourage one another and build each other up, just as in fact you are doing" (1 Thessalonians 5:11).

As an encourager you may not guarantee playing time for yourself, but you can be sure that God is aware of all that you do, and He will reward you for your faithfulness!

Day 2
Filling Your Role
Have you ever heard of anybody that dreamed of sitting on the bench? Of course not! Everyone dreams of being the "star player," the one who hits the grand slam to win the game, or shoots the basket at the buzzer to send the game into overtime. Nobody *wants* to sit on the bench. Unfortunately, unless you attend a very small school, there are usually too many players for everyone to be a starter, or to even play every game. One of the most difficult tasks for any coach is to decide which players to use. Whether you are the star player or rarely get to take off your warm-ups, you have a role on your team.

Read 1 Corinthians 12:12-31 and answer the following:

Which part of the body does it say is the most important?

How might an attitude of superiority arise among certain members of the body? (v. 21)

On your team, do you tend to identify more with someone who is superior or inferior? Why?

Attitudes of superiority can develop based on athletic ability, appearance, race, gender, religion, or social status. All of us have talents and abilities. They may not be athletic. They may be musical, artistic, literary, or scientific. In athletics, there is rarely a team of all-stars. Usually one or two players stand out as the "most athletic" or "best players." They usually get most of the attention. If you are one of the best players on your team, you know what it's like to be expected to play well every game, to help the team to the playoffs, or to make the all-star roster. Chances are most of you reading this can identify more with the "average" player, the one who shows up to practice, works hard for two hours, and hopes to play during the game next week. Who is more important, the star or the average player? Actually, both are important. Some teams need a "star" to push other players to be their best. Some teams play better together when everyone is "average." The key is for everyone on the team to play their best all the time, not just when they have a chance to play or to win the game.

What would you say is your role on the team?

Are you satisfied with your role? Why or why not?

Read verses 22-26 in 1 Corinthians again and write down how you can make every member of the body feel special, regardless of their role:

There is a difference between accepting your role on the team while continuing to work hard and develop the skills necessary to work your way into the lineup, and developing bitterness toward the coach and resentment toward those who play ahead of you. When a player does not accept her role on the team she may develop envy, jealousy, pride, and even bitterness. It is difficult to watch the success of others when you are wanting and working for the same thing for yourself.

The Parable of the Talents
Have you ever compared what you have to what someone else has? It is a natural tendency we have to judge ourselves or what we have based on what we see in others' lives. The problem is, comparison usually leads to inferiority. Sooner or later, we find someone who has more than we do.

Read Matthew 25:14-30. This story is often referred to as the parable of the talents. A parable is a story that is told to help get a point across. In this parable, the talents are a type of money that was used in Jesus' time. The master entrusts different amounts to each of his servants.

Why does the master do this? (Read vv. 14 and 15 again.)

If you had been the third servant, how would you respond to only receiving one talent when the others had more?

The master makes it clear in verses 19-23 that he is pleased with how faithful the servants are with what they are given, not how they did in comparison to each other. In a way, God is like the master. God gives each of us certain abilities and responsibilities in life, desires us to be faithful with what He gives us, and wants us to share in his happiness (eternal life); in other words, to use what we are given for God's glory. Unlike the master, God looks at more than just the outcome. He desires to know what our motive is.

Can you think of a time when you were envious of someone? What were you envious of?

Did your envy prevent you from developing the abilities or talents you were given? How?

The Missing Link
One college coach used to tell her players that "a team is only as strong as its weakest link." In other words, the "weakest" player determines how good the team will be, because she will influence how hard the rest of the team works, and whether or not they are challenged to get better!

The Bible is clear on how we are to handle situations in which we may be tempted to take it easy or "coast" during practice. Read Colossians 3:23 and write down what your motivation as a Christian is to be, whether you are in the starting lineup or sitting on the bench:

Do you do your best during every practice? Every drill? Why or why not?

Do the other players on your team do their best every practice?

How do you think this affects the team?

How can you challenge yourself to give 100% at every practice and every game?

How can you challenge your teammates to give 100% at every practice and every game?

TIME OUT!
Is there a teammate that you are envious of? Do you believe that your coach is wrong in not playing you, or have you found yourself thinking about quitting the team because you don't get to play as much as you think you should? It might be that you are wrestling with the issue of pride. Pride often prevents us from viewing situations realistically. Pride is at the root of many sins, and it will not help you to improve yourself athletically or spiritually.

Consider the friendship of Jonathan and David. Jonathan was King Saul's son, and the rightful heir to the throne. One day Jonathan met David, a local shepherd, and Jonathan recognized right away that David had certain qualities and characteristics that would make David a better king! At that time, Jonathan could have been jealous and tried to get David in trouble, or even killed him so that David would not take away his throne, but he didn't. In 1 Samuel 18, you can read the story of Jonathan and David.

Take some time right now to pray and ask God to search your heart. Confess to Him any thoughts of jealousy, envy or pride that you have had. Ask Him to forgive you and to help you develop thoughts about yourself and others that are encouraging and loving.

Day 3
Unity
If you have ever been part of an athletic team, you know how exciting it can be when everyone is playing well together. Plays are run the way they're supposed to be, teammates perform at their best, and it seems like the whole team is in unison. Nothing can go wrong! However, there are also those times when players seem to do their own thing, nothing goes right, and everyone leaves the game or practice frustrated. In his book *The Handbook on Athletic Perfection*, Wes Neal describes two keys to team unity.[1] To be successful, a team needs a **common purpose** and **team spirit.**

A common purpose, or goal, means that everyone is working together to achieve the goal. The goal might be the league championship, a winning season, or even winning a single game during the season! Often teams don't have a common goal, and

Relationships as an Athlete

players are focused on individual goals such as being high scorer for the game, winning MVP of the league, or making the all-state team. Individual goals are necessary, but in team sports they are most effective when they are consistent with team goals.

What are your team goals for this season?

What are your individual goals for this season?

Are your goals consistent with the team goals? Could your individual goals prevent the team goals from happening in any way? If so, you may need to reevaluate your individual goals.

TIME OUT!
Take some time to evaluate where you are at in each of the following areas. Circle the number that best describes how you feel about that area of your life at this time according to this table: Very Dissatisfied = 1; Dissatisfied = 2; Neutral = 3; Satisfied = 4; and Very Satisfied = 5.

Athletics	1	2	3	4	5
Family	1	2	3	4	5
School	1	2	3	4	5
Social	1	2	3	4	5
Spiritual	1	2	3	4	5

Did you say that you were very dissatisfied or dissatisfied in any of the areas? If so, take some time to think and pray about what you would like to be different in that area. Write your goal for each area in the space provided.

Athletics:

Family:

School:

Social:

Spiritual:

Team Spirit

Did you ever hear the cheer, "We've got spirit, yes we do, we've got spirit, how about you?" Fans and cheerleaders of opposing teams chant this cheer to see which side has the most spirit. As a Christian athlete, you have the potential to help your team develop THE ULTIMATE team spirit. Wes Neal describes team spirit in this way:[1]

"Team spirit empowered by human emotions will be inconsistent. Only that empowered by God will be consistent." (Read James 1:17)

"Actions are a better teacher than words alone in communicating team spirit to other teammates." (Read James 2:17)

Team spirit must begin with you. This type of team spirit

Relationships as an Athlete

includes allowing your actions to be controlled by the Holy Spirit (Ephesians 5:18). This includes good sportsmanship, avoiding "cheap fouls" or other plays which are out of frustration or lack of self-control. It also means using your words to inspire others, not swearing at the officials or opponents, and encouraging others rather than yelling at them for making a mistake. It is often difficult to do this in the middle of a game when everyone is tense and the adrenaline is flowing. However, this is exactly when we are to demonstrate that we are controlled by the Holy Spirit–when it is most difficult!

Name three ways you can demonstrate this type of team spirit:

1.

2.

3.

The Apostle Paul knew that the reality of Christian living must be seen in him so others could have an example to follow. (Read 1 Corinthians 4:16.) The best witness for your coach, teammates, fans, and anyone else is how you act both on and off the court.

Day 4
Hurdles Teams Face
There are several hurdles that can interfere with team spirit and

unity. These hurdles can prevent a team from reaching its potential and can often destroy relationships among team members. Examples of these hurdles are jealousy, cliques, gossip, impatience, lack of commitment/discipline, selfishness, and pride.

Jealousy arises out of our sinful nature (Galatians 5:17-21) and means to be resentfully envious. You may admire the abilities of a teammate, but if you resent her for having her abilities or talents or feel less useful yourself because you don't "measure up," you are jealous of that person and need to confess that sin to God. Otherwise, your jealousy may impair your ability to play with that person and that will affect the team's unity.

Cliques (pronounced "clicks") involve "in-groups," and usually serve to meet the need for belonging and friendship. Unfortunately, cliques by nature tend to leave someone out of the group. Cliques are different than close friendships because they seek to leave out certain individuals who don't "fit in" with the group. It is possible that your team is seen as a clique by other students if you spend time outside of your sport with only your teammates, or look down on others if they aren't part of the team. Sometimes cliques develop within a team, and can divide the team. Older players may not associate outside of practice and games with younger players.

Gossip is another issue that can sometimes cause conflict between team members. There are two words for gossip in the Old Testament. The first is the Hebrew word *nirgan*, and it means "to roll to pieces." The second is also a Hebrew word, *rakiyl*, which means "traveling" with a confidence. Gossip can not only mean sharing information that was given to you with the other person's trust that you wouldn't repeat it, but it can

Relationships as an Athlete 171

also indicate a desire or intent to intentionally hurt another– "roll them to pieces." Gossip includes situations such as sharing what someone said about another person with that person, or helping spread rumors, or telling a lie about someone else to "get back" at them. The Bible is very clear on how damaging gossip can be (Proverbs 11:13; 16:28; 20:19).

A **lack of commitment/discipline** usually occurs when not everyone on the team has the same goal. Some players may only be on the team because they wanted to be with their friends, or their parents wanted them to play. Others are always working hard to improve and play their best. Some athletes are very dedicated in their sport, but are very lackadaisical in the classroom. This lack of discipline in other areas of life is a problem because self-discipline is a trait that needs to be evident in every area of your life.

When a player is **selfish**, she is more likely to focus on gaining attention and praise for herself, even if it means the team not doing as well. She may believe that she is the only one who can win the game, or that the team cannot win without her. Selfishness is most obvious in actions. A selfish player is less likely to pass the ball, blames others for her mistakes, and makes decisions that jeopardize the team, such as breaking team rules. Selfishness in one player often results in resentment in one or more other players. A selfish player is more concerned with how she plays than how the team does.

Conflict between team members is usually unavoidable. During the course of a season it is likely that arguments or disagreements about something will occur between two or more members of a given team. The problems with team conflicts is that it usually does not just affect the individuals involved, but generally will broaden to include other members of the team. This can lead to bruised egos, wounded feelings, and frustration among team members. Sometimes the conflict carries over into practice or game situations, and team performance is affected.

Pride can mean to take delight in one's own or another's achievements, or self-respect. Pride can also mean to have an unduly high opinion of oneself, or an attitude of arrogance. Most athletes have a sense of pride about themselves and their team, and this sense of pride motivates athletes to practice hard and to continue to improve in an effort to demonstrate that hard work to others. However, you can probably think of a teammate or opponent who fits the second definition. While athletics can help individuals develop positive traits such as a healthy respect for self and others, the competitive nature of athletics and the reality that in most sports there is a "winner" and a "loser" sometimes results in a prideful attitude. It is fine to have a sense of self-respect and worth because of who you are in your relationship with Christ, but the Bible warns us about the kind of pride that develops an arrogant attitude and elevates us in our own minds (Proverbs 11:2; 13:10; 16:18). Instead, we are told to look out for the interests of others and not to place ourselves above other people (Philippians 2:3).

Which of the hurdles mentioned do you struggle with the most? Place an "I" in the blank next to that hurdle. Which of the hurdles does your team struggle with as a group? Place a "T" next to that hurdle.

____Jealousy
____Selfishness
____Pride
____Gossip
____Cliques
____Conflict
____Other _____

Exercises to Build Team Strength

Accountability helps to insure that everyone is committed to the same goals and following team rules. Prayer partners is one way to help keep accountability. Team members that are interested can pray with a teammate(s) during the season. They can get together on a regular basis, either before or after practice, before classes, or on the weekend. Use the time to pray for each other, your coach, the team, and your opponents. It will help you to stay focused on God during competition and to be aware of the hurdles that may trip you up.

Sometimes the hurdles mentioned can damage relationships, even between teammates. When this happens, it is important to remember that as a Christian, you can seek *reconciliation*, especially if the damaged relationship is between you and another Christian. Reconciliation is the process of restoring a relationship that has been damaged or broken. If another Christian has offended you in some way (gossiped about you, said something hurtful/unflattering, etc.), the Bible says that you are to go to the person privately and discuss the problem with her (Matthew 18:15). Be careful not to complain to others about the person. If you do, you are committing the sin of gossip (Proverbs 11:13; 2 Corinthians 12:20) and may draw others into an argument/conflict that they have nothing to do with (Proverbs 16:28; 26:20). If you discuss the matter with the other person and they are repentant, you may forgive them and your relationship is restored. If they respond inappropriately, minimize what happened, or flat out deny they did anything wrong, you may choose to either bring along a witness who heard the person/saw what happened, or use an objective "mediator" that can help sort out the conflict between the two of you.

Reconciliation does not necessarily mean that you will be good friends with the person or have the same type of relationship you did in the past. Trust may be broken between the two of you. As Christians we are called to "live at peace with one another" as much as possible (Romans 12:17-19) so that others may see the witness of the body of Christ. In this way, you demonstrate servanthood by looking out for the interests of others ahead of your own, and helping to create unity within the body of Christ. Remember from the section on forgiveness that we are called to forgive others regardless of how they respond to us!

Are there any relationships in your life that are damaged or broken?

What happened?

Ask God to forgive you for any bitterness, jealousy, or hatred you may have towards this person. Take some time to pray and consider if you need to ask the other person's forgiveness for anything. The steps to reconciliation include asking forgiveness from God and others when you have sinned against them. You may need to go directly to the person and ask for her forgiveness. Remember, if you ask forgiveness and the other person does not give it, you have done what you need to. It may take time before the other person is ready to forgive, but you have laid the groundwork. Continue to pray for her. If the person does grant forgiveness, you may slowly start to rebuild the relationship if that is what you both want. Otherwise, continue to follow God's directives in your own life. Don't try to "force" the relationship. Even with forgiveness, some wounds heal more slowly than others.

Day 5
Part One
Leadership
Have you ever sat on the bench wanting to get into the game? Have you ever dreamed of being the one on the field who scores the game-winning goal, or serves an ace to win the match, or catches the person ahead of you at the finish line to win the race? We all have dreams of being the hero, of stepping up to face the challenge and making things happen. Those dreams are part of the competitive drive: to be the best and to win at whatever sport you are playing.

Whether or not you are one of the stars on the team, you play an important role. The star player isn't always the leader. On any team, it is important to have both good leaders and good followers. Name someone you know personally or a public figure whom you consider to be a good leader:

What is it about that person that makes him/her a good leader?

Sometimes leaders are thought of as the most popular, best-looking, best-dressed, or smartest people. However, leadership goes beyond physical appearance or how well-liked you are by others. True leadership involves qualities that have nothing to do with attractiveness or appearance, but rather how that person relates to others.

Take a few moments to think about your team. Write down the names of the player(s) you consider to be the leaders on your team.

What makes that person a leader?

All teams must have both good leaders and good followers. You need to know what role you have on your team. For the sake of this study, we will concentrate on the leadership role.

When we talk about leadership on the team, we are talking about more than just who is the best player or athlete. Leadership requires much more than athleticism. Leadership is having the ability to influence others. A leader is someone who leads the team by example in the areas of motivation, discipline, and character. You might ask, "What does that look like?"

Let's look at some examples of leadership in the Bible. Read the following passages and list some of the qualities that make up a good leader.

Relationships as an Athlete

Joseph (Genesis 39:4-10)

Daniel (Daniel 1:5-8; 2:14; 6:1-10)

Deborah (Judges 4:4, 5)

David (Acts 13:22)

Now list some of the qualities that make up a bad leader.

Ahab (1 Kings 16:30-33)

Jezebel (1 Kings 21:25)

Saul (1 Samuel 13:5-14; 15:1-26)

As Christians, we are to follow the example of Jesus in all that we do. He is our role model for the Christian life. He is the One who leads and guides us. He also gives us an example of a perfect leader. He always does what God tells Him to do. He has the big picture of what is best for the whole world, not just what is best for Him or for a few people.

Read the following verses and write down the characteristics that describe the life of Jesus:

John 10:3-4; 10:11; 10:14, 15

Philippians 2:3-8

Matthew 20:28

TIME OUT!
Let's review what you have learned so far about the qualities of a leader. If God calls you to be a leader or places you in a leadership position on your team, what kind of qualities should be evident in your life?

Servant leadership
Jesus said, "*If anyone wants to be first, he must be the very last, and the servant of all*" (Mark 9:35). The best way to learn to be a leader is to first learn how to serve others. There are opportunities every day to serve those around you, whether it is helping pick up after practice or doing extra chores to help out at home. Leadership is one of the most critical areas of team strength. While strong leadership can motivate and encourage others, a lack of leadership can hinder a team. Often team captains are selected because they are respected by other players. The other team members follow their lead. Sometimes the leaders on the

team do not have an actual title like "captain"—they are more of a natural leader that others respond to and follow. Leadership is a very critical part of any team. Leaders will make mistakes like everyone else, but if they mislead others or are unwilling to submit to their authority, there will be problems for everyone who follows them.

"Whoever would find herself at the top must be willing to lose herself at the bottom." –Unknown

Part Two
Listening to the Coach
"I can't believe she didn't put me in! We could have won that game!"
"Why do we have to listen to him anyway? We could probably coach ourselves better without him!"

Have you ever listened to athletes complain about their coach? It's always easy to judge decisions the coach has made after the game is finished. Most players don't agree with absolutely everything their coach says or does. However, the difference between the players and the coach is **authority**. The coach is in a position of leadership and has authority over the players. The players don't have authority over the coach.

Laura was playing on a team which had a brand new coach. The problem was, everyone liked the former coach and wanted her to stay. The school administrators felt it was best to hire someone different for the position. The players didn't agree. That year with the new coach was the toughest Laura ever had as an athlete. Why? Because sometimes it was hard to tell who actually had the authority! The team would ignore the coach, not run the plays she asked them to, and even talked about the coach behind her back. This was not obedience to authority; it was more like mutiny!

It is important to remember that whether or not you agree with your coach, God asks you to obey him or her. *"Everyone must submit [herself] to the governing authorities, for there is no authority except that which God has established. The authorities that exist have been established by God. Consequently, [she] who rebels against the authority is rebelling against what God has instituted…"* (Romans 13:1-2).

There is a difference between obedience and submission. Obedience has to do with *actions*, while submission has to do with *attitude*. If you constantly rebel against your coach, show up to practice late, break team rules, "cop an attitude," or argue with what you're told to do, you will probably have consequences from your coach for your disobedience. But God is also concerned with your attitude. When you rebel against authority, it is because you are exalting yourself, trying to place yourself in the position of authority. What you are really doing is rebelling against God.

You might say, "But you don't know my coach! She swears at us all the time, makes us run sprints just because she's in a bad mood, and she never even played the game herself!" You're right, I don't know your coach, but I do know the One who placed her in that position, and God is asking you to trust *Him*. Coaches make mistakes. Everyone does. Everyone but God.

As we mentioned earlier, each player on the team has a role. That role may change each season, depending on whether the player develops and matures. Some players think more highly of themselves than they ought to, and this can often lead to jealousy among teammates. The player may not accept her role because she believes she is being "cheated" by the coach. Marcie is an example. Marcie was a third-string goalie on the soccer team. Although she was a decent player and a fairly good athlete, Marcie was not as talented as the two players ahead of her. Marcie had a difficult time accepting this because her parents and friends were constantly complaining that the coach was "not giving a fair chance" to Marcie and was "playing favorites."

When Marcie went to confront her coach, she had a chip on her shoulder. Rather than respecting the coach's authority, Marcie tried to tell the coach how to do her job. Marcie told the coach all the reasons why she should be the first-string goalie. The coach looked Marcie in the eye and said, "Well, Marcie, maybe you aren't as good as you think you are." Not many coaches are as blunt as Marcie's was. It doesn't help to damage someone's ego, but there are times when players need to be told the truth and reminded that they are not the ones in charge. Even if everyone around you believes that you are the best player on the team, the coach is the one who decides which players get in the game.

TIME OUT!
Who are the people in authority over you?

How do you respond to that authority (do you listen to what the coach says and follow rules, or "buck the system" and complain behind his/her back)?

There may be a situation in which someone in authority asks you to do something that is contrary to what the Bible states. Even then, it is important to check your attitude (Psalm 66:18), communicate your convictions, and commit to obey God first! God will take care of you. He can give you the grace to endure the situation you are in, change the heart of those in authority, or provide a way out of the situation. If you believe that you are to disobey a coach out of obedience to God, keep in mind that you need to be willing to take the consequences of your disobedience. The story of Daniel is a good example. Read Daniel 6:1-28.

How did Daniel disobey the King?

Why did Daniel disobey?

What was the consequence for his disobedience?

How did God intervene in the situation?

How to respond to a difficult coach
All coaches aren't Christians, and even the ones that are aren't perfect. What can you do if you don't agree with something your coach has said or done? The first thing to do is to **pray** for wisdom (James 1:5). **Check** your own attitude and motivation,

and make sure that you are being obedient as a player. Read the Bible for direction on what God wants you to do in your particular situation (Psalm 119:11). **Consult** with a parent, friend, pastor, or Bible study leader for direction on how to handle the situation (Proverbs 15:22; 27:9).

Check your attitude. If you want to prove the coach wrong or try to get others "on your side," there may be issues of pride getting in the way. Comments such as "I deserve to play" and "You owe me" reflect an attitude of entitlement. Remember, your coach chose you as a member of the team. Your job is to trust in the coach's authority.

If your coach is not a Christian but is willing to discuss the situation with you, be a witness. It doesn't matter that you are younger than your coach. First Timothy 4:12 says, *"Don't let anyone look down on you because you are young, but set an example for the believers in speech, in life, in love, in faith and in purity."* Show respect for your coach's authority, even if you don't agree with what the coach does or says. Conversely, he or she may not agree with or understand your perspective.

If you have done everything possible to resolve the issue/problem between you and your coach, consider your next step very carefully. Quitting the team may be an easy way out of a difficult situation, but it may not be what God would want you to do. Every situation is unique. If your problem is related to dissatisfaction with playing time, the coach's strategy, or other coaching decisions, you need to make sure that you are first submitting to the coach's authority. However, there may be situations in which you need to go to the coach's authority (e.g., athletic director or school official) with the problem (such as a coach buying alcohol for players, dating a player, or a coach being physically or verbally abusive to players). Keep in mind that others may not agree with you or might even ignore the problem. The most important thing is to be obedient to what God asks you to do (1 John 3:23, 24; 2 John 6).

Be an example on your team. Rather than joining in the complaints others have, show the proper response to authority. You will be amazed at how your teammates (and your coach) will notice! Memorize verses on authority to help direct and encourage you during difficult times. Here are a few suggestions:

Romans 13:1

Ephesians 6:5, 6

Colossians 3:22

1 Thessalonians 5:12, 13

Titus 3:1

1 Peter 2:13, 14

Player-Coach Relationships
Since we have placed such an emphasis on leadership and the importance of the coach's authority, it is important to also consider the kind of relationship a player has with the coach. By the time an athlete is in high school, she is likely to spend more time

with her coach during the season than she will interacting with her parent(s)! Most athletes respect and admire their coaches. The coach is in a position to serve as a role model, an encourager, and a teacher during a very formative time in an athlete's life. In fact, coaches were some of the most influential people in the lives of the women who have written this study. Many coaches have a close friendship with players, especially in the role of mentor. However, it is difficult for a coach to have an intimate friendship with a player on the team because of the difference in roles between a coach and a player. Since the coach is in a position of authority, he or she has power in the relationship. The coach can make decisions that affect the player's role and position on the team. Therefore, it is never an "equal" relationship while the player is on the team. Even if the coach and player are close in age, it can be confusing to the player as well as other members of the team if the coach has an intimate friendship with a player.

This is not to say that coaches and players can never be friends or that relationships can't change as the player gets older and graduates. It is possible, however, for a player to misinterpret feelings of admiration and respect for the coach as something more. In the section on "Relationships as a Female," we looked at what can happen when there is not balance in relationships. It is possible for a player to have an inappropriate relationship with a coach. It may be an emotionally dependent relationship, or a physical/sexual relationship. In any case, such a relationship is not appropriate. In most states, sexual relations between an adult and a minor is illegal, even if both "want" the relationship and "consent" to it. It is the coach's responsibility to balance his/her life so that he/she has other relationships outside of the team. It is also important for you to develop other healthy relationships, both on the team and outside of athletics. This will help you to grow and develop relationally and emotionally as well as spiritually.

TIME OUT!
What should you do if you suspect that one of your teammates is involved with a coach? It is not a good idea to walk around making unfounded accusations. Remember that when you say something about another person, you may not intend to "hurt" the person you are talking about, but gossip usually leads to damaged relationships and reputations. If you are upset at Coach Smith because he seems to favor your teammate, Erin, don't assume that there is something "going on" between Erin and Coach Smith. Rather, talk to Coach Smith about the perceived preferential treatment. If you actually witness something physical/sexual between a coach and a player, or if another player tells you firsthand that something is going on, then you may need to tell another adult. Pray for wisdom as to how to handle the situation. Don't run and tell other teammates or friends because that may lead to other rumors or gossip. Keep the number of people involved limited. Discuss the matter with a parent, school counselor, teacher, principal, or athletic director. Let the adults in the situation handle it.

Wrap Up

Congratulations! You made it! Hopefully this book challenged you to examine both your identity as a female Christian athlete and your relationships with God and with others. Remember, your identity is reflected in your actions. Can others tell that you are a Christian by how you play? Are there other areas of your life that do not reflect your identity as a Christian? As an athlete, others will watch you, maybe even admire you for what you do. That might seem overwhelming, but not if you are depending on God.

Completing this study is just the beginning. There are additional resources listed in the Appendix that you are encouraged to check out. Ministry organizations such as the Fellowship of Christian Athletes and Athletes in Action may have a huddle or representative at your school. Contact them and get connected with other athletes who live and play for Jesus. Participating in athletics can help you to develop perseverance, commitment, confidence, and the ability to work as part of a team. These are qualities that will not just make you a better athlete, but will equip you to be your best in your studies, job, family relationships, and just about every other area of life. Blessings to you as you continue to grow in your relationship with Christ. May the Lord continue to mold you into the woman He desires you to be!

"…he who began a good work in you will carry it on to completion until the day of Christ Jesus."

Philippians 1:6

References

Chapter 1–Identity as a Christian

1. Dobson, James. *Life on the Edge.* Dallas: Word Publishing, 1995.

2. George, Bob. *Classic Christianity.* Eugene, OR: Harvest House Publishers, 1989.

3. Sanders, Oswald. *Enjoying Intimacy With God.* Chicago: Moody Press, 1980.

4. Hybels, Bill. *Too Busy Not to Pray.*

5. Arthur, Kay. *Lord, Teach Me to Pray.* Chattanooga, TN: Precept Ministries of Reach Out, Inc. 1982.

Chapter 2–Identity as a Female

1. Evans, Mary J. *Women in the Bible.* Downers Grove, IL: InterVarsity Press, 1983.

2. Van Leeuwen, Mary Stewart. *Gender and Grace.* Downers Grove, IL: InterVarsity Press, 1990.

3. Howard, Jeanette. *Out of Egypt: Leaving Lesbianism Behind.* Crowborough, England: Monarch Publications; Baltimore, MD: Regeneration Books, 1991.

4. McDowell, Josh. *Handbook on Counseling Youth.* Dallas: Word Publishing, 1996.

5. Santucci, Patricia. "Facts About Eating Disorders." National Eating Disorder Screening Project Educational Presentation. 1998.

6. Powers, Pauline S. "Athletes and Eating Disorders." National Eating Disorder Screening Project Educational Presentation, 1998.

7. U.S. Olympic Committee Sports Medicine Council, International Center for Sports Nutrition, and University of Nebraska Medical Center Eating Disorders Program. "Eating Disorders." 1993.

8. Tucker, Ruth, and Liefield, Walter. *Daughters of the Church.* Grand Rapids, MI: Zondervan, 1987.

9. Sayers, Dorothy. *Are Women Human?* Grand Rapids, MI: Eerdmans, 1971.

10. Anderson, Neil. *The Bondage Breaker.* Eugene, OR: Harvest House Publishers, 1993.

References

Chapter 3–Identity as an Athlete

1. Yantis, Wendy Kafouy. "The Competitive Woman." *Athletes in Action* 1992.

2. Drollinger, Karen. *Grace and Glory*. Waco, TX: Word Books, 1990.

3. RecoveryWorks.com

4. Vine, W. E., Unger, M. F., and White, W. *Vine's Expository Dictionary of Biblical Words*. Nashville: Thomas Nelson Publishers, 1985.

Chapter 4–Relationships as a Christian

1. Hufstetler, James. "On Knowing Oneself." *The Banner of Truth* Jan. 1987: 13.

2. Bridges, Jerry. *Trusting God*. Colorado Springs, CO: NavPress, 1988.

3. Flynn, Leslie B. *Great Church Fights*. Wheaton, IL: Victor Books, 1976.

4. Seamands, David. *Healing for Damaged Emotions*. Wheaton, IL: Scripture Press Publications, 1981.

5. Swindoll, Charles. *Improving Your Serve*. Waco, TX: Word Books, 1981.

6. Pippert, Rebecca. *Out of the Salt Shaker and into the World*. Downers Grove, IL: InterVarsity Press, 1979.

Chapter 5–Relationships as a Female

1. White, Jerry, and White, Mary. *Friends and Friendship: The Secrets of Drawing Closer.* Colorado Springs, CO: NavPress, 1982.

2. Howard, Jeanette. *Out of Egypt: Leaving Lesbianism Behind.* Crowborough, England: Monarch Publications; Baltimore, MD: Regeneration Books, 1991.

3. Davies, Bob, and Rentzel, Lori. *Coming Out of Homosexuality: New Freedom for Men and Women.* Downers Grove, IL: InterVarsity Press, 1993.

4. Dallas, Joe. *Desires in Conflict: Answering the Struggle for Sexual Identity.* Eugene, OR: Harvest House Publishers, 1991.

Chapter 6–Relationships as an Athlete

1. Neal, Wes. *The Handbook on Athletic Perfection.* Grand Island, NE: Cross Training Publishing, 1999.

Appendix

Abortion
Michels, Nancy. *Helping Women Recover from Abortion.* Minneapolis: Bethany House Publishers, 1988.

Abuse
Allender, Dan. *The Wounded Heart.* Colorado Springs, CO: NavPress, 1990.

Heitritter, Lynn, and Vought, Jeanette. *Helping Victims of Sexual Abuse.* Minneapolis: Bethany House Publishers, 1989.

Scott, Kay. *Sexual Assault: Will I Ever Feel Okay Again?* Minneapolis: Bethany House Publishers, 1993.

Seamands, David. *Healing for Damaged Emotions.* Scripture Press Publications, Inc., 1981.

Athletics
Drollinger, Karen. *Grace and Glory.* Waco, TX: Word Books, 1990.

Neal, Wes. *The Handbook on Athletic Perfection*. Grand Island, NE: Cross Training Publishing, 1981.

Thiessen, Gordon. *The Athlete's Topical Bible*. Grand Island, NE: Cross Training Publishing, 1993.

Thiessen, Gordon. *Cross Training Manual: Playbook for Christian Athletes*. Grand Island, NE: Cross Training Publishing, 1991.

Dating

Burgen, Jim. *What's the Big Deal? About sex: Loving God's way*. Cincinnati, OH: Standard Publishing, 1999.

Harris, Joshua. *I Kissed Dating Goodbye*. Sisters, OR: Multnomah Publishers, Inc., 1997.

Young, Ben, and Adams, Sam. *The 10 Commandments of Dating*. Nashville, TN: Thomas Nelson Publishers, 1999.

True Love Waits
1-800-LUV-WAIT
www.truelovewaits.com

Drugs and Alcohol

One Way to Play–Drug Free
8701 Leeds Road
Kansas City, MO 64129
816-921-0909
www.fca.org

Appendix

Teen Challenge
www.teenchallenge.com

Eating Disorders
Books:
Rowland, Cynthia Joyce. *The Monster Within: Overcoming Bulimia.* 1984.

Beyond the Looking Glass: Daily Devotions for Overcoming Anorexia and Bulimia. By staff and patients at Remuda Ranch. 1992.

Jantz, Gregory L. *Hope, Help & Healing for Eating Disorders.* 1995.

Drs. Frank Minirth, Paul Meier, Robert Helmfelt, Sharon Sneed and Don Hawkins. *Love Hunger.* Columbine, NY: Fawcett, 1990.

Organizations:
International Center for Sports Nutrition
502 South 44th Street, Room 3012
Omaha, NE 68105-1065
402-559-5505

Remuda Ranch
One East Apache
Wickenburg, AZ 85390
1-800-445-1900
www.remuda-ranch.com

EDAP Eating Disorders Awareness & Prevention
603 Stewart St., Suite 803
Seattle, WA 98101
206-382-3587

Homosexuality
Books:
Comiskey, Andy. *Pursuing Sexual Wholeness.* Creation House, 1989.

Dallas, Joe. *Desires in Conflict: Answering the Struggle for Sexual Identity.* Eugene, OR: Harvest House Publishers, 1991.

Davies, Bob, and Rentzel, Lori. *Coming Out of Homosexuality.* Downers Grove, IL: InterVarsity Press, 1993.

McClung, Floyd. *The Father Heart of God.* Eugene, OR: Harvest House Publishers, 1985.

Satinover, Dr. Jeffrey. *Homosexuality and the Politics of Truth.* Grand Rapids, MI: Baker Books, 1996.

Whitehead, Neil, and Briar. *My Genes Made Me Do It! A Scientific Look at Sexual Orientation.*

Ministries:
Desert Stream Ministries
P.O. Box 7635
Anaheim, CA 92817
714-779-6899
www.desertstream.org

His Heart Ministries
12162 E. Mississippi Ave.
P.O. Box 12321
Aurora, CO 80011
303-369-2961

Exodus International
P.O. Box 77652
Seattle, WA 98177
206-784-7799
www.exodus.base.org

Relationship Issues
Cloud, Henry, and Townsend, John. *Boundaries.* Grand Rapids, MI: Zondervan, 1992.

Handley, Rod. *Character Counts–Who's Counting Yours? A Guide for Accountability Groups.* Grand Island, NE: Cross Training Publishing, 1999.

Cloud, Henry, and Townsend, John. *Safe People.* Grand Rapids, MI: Zondervan, 1995.

Sports Ministries
Athletes in Action

Competitive Edge International Ministry
P.O. Box 3960
Mission Viejo, CA 92690
714-44-3614
www.ceisports.org

Fellowship of Christian Athletes
8701 Leeds Road
Kansas City, MO 64129
816-921-0909
www.fca.org

International Sports Federation
P.O. Box 13038
Arlington, TX 76094
1-800-999-3113 Ext. 151
TEAMISF@AOL.COM

Sports Outreach America
www.sportsoutreach.org